The Collegeville Concise Glossary of Biblical Terms

Dianne Bergant, C.S.A.

A Liturgical Press Book

THE LITURGICAL PRESS
Collegeville, Minnesota

1	2	3	4	5	6	7	8	9

Library of Congress Cataloging-in-Publication Data

Bergant, Dianne.
    The Collegeville concise glossary of biblical terms / Dianne Bergant.
      p.   cm.
    Includes index.
    ISBN 0-8146-2239-9
    1. Bible—Dictionaries. I. Title.
BS440.B464 1994
220.3—dc20   93-31852
                                     CIP

Contents

Preface

This book grew out of a series of disparate short articles that appeared over several years in *The Bible Today* as a feature entitled **"Bible Terms Today."** It is a response to a suggestion made by Michael Glazier that these articles be collected and expanded. While most of the original articles appear in these pages in revised form, the bulk of the material is original.

The arrangement of the book follows the order of the Roman Catholic canon. Each article, while discrete in itself, is intended to afford the reader a way into the thought of the respective biblical book. The articles provide insight into major theological themes (e.g., **Flesh, Spirit**), literary information that will aid in reading biblical material (e.g., **Myth, Legend**), or explanations of some troublesome concepts (e.g., **Day of the LORD**). The information in each article is seldom germane exclusively to that particular biblical book (e.g., **Flesh** and **Spirit** are important in Romans as well as in Corinthians); thus one entry can throw light on the material of several books.

These articles were written for the educated reader who is serious about biblical inquiry but is not a specialist in the field. Besides acting as introductions to the biblical books, they can also be used to enhance the knowledge the reader already enjoys, serving as a resource for those involved in study groups as well as for those responsible for homiletic preparation.

For the convenience of the reader, the **Contents** lists the articles according to biblical book, while the **Index** lists them alphabetically.

GENESIS—MYTH, LEGEND

One feature which we almost immediately note as we read the Book of Genesis is the often imaginative and exaggerated character of its expression. The human beings appear to be more than human; the gods are portrayed as less than divine; the animals act in ways that far surpass their natures. Surely here we are reading something more than history or natural science. But if we say that what is written is not verified history, or an empirical fact, we do not mean that it is not true. There are important, recognized ways to express truth other than by means of history or science. Myths and legends can also convey profound truths.

Myth

As understood in the ancient Near East, a myth is usually a story about gods or other supernatural beings. It tends to interpret what is real in terms of the ideal. Because it is a story about gods, its setting is typically a world other than the world of ordinary human beings. While it is true that human beings often play significant roles, the lead characters are always divine. This explains what might otherwise be considered exaggeration. When talking about a god, especially one's own god, only superlatives are in order.

In studying the writings of biblical Israel, scholars have been able to discover parallels with and allusions to the myths of neighboring societies. For example, Egypt had a tradition, not unlike the narrative found in Genesis 2, wherein a potter-god created humankind. Mesopotamia told about a tree of life, a serpent who tricked a man in search of immortality, winged cherubs stationed outside of a garden sanctuary, and a great flood that covered the entire world and from which one family was saved.

One cannot help wondering: Was Israel influenced by its neighbors or did they all draw from a common stock of ancient traditions? Did Israel believe that the myth was the reality? Was there, in fact, any other way to speak of reality? However we answer these questions, it is important to understand that Israel was as concerned about truth as we are. Perhaps our ancestors were not as bound to one way of expressing it as we seem to be. They certainly appear to have been more comfortable with poetry and imaginative imagery than are we.

Legend

A second literary form that is prominent in Genesis is the legend. This is usually a fanciful tale about some factual person, event, or thing. Like the myth, the legend is filled with exaggeration and imaginative flourishes intended to illustrate just how important a subject is to the community. Although this may appear to be an unwarranted distortion, such is not the case. People, events, and things that are important to us often take on dimensions that are unrecognized by others outside of our circles.

The stories of Abraham and Sarah and of the other ancestors are frequently legendary (cf. Gen 12–50). Their grounding in history is not to be denied, but the historical accuracy of every detail of the narrative is surely to be questioned. Heroes such as Noah were remembered by means of legends. There are also etiological legends, delightful explanations of why things are the way they are. For example, the story of Lot's wife explains the presence of pillars of salt in the Judean desert.

Realizing that truth can be expressed in many different ways, we must be most attentive to particular literary forms with their distinct methods and purposes so that we can better discover the message of a story, a message often as profound as it is hidden.

EXODUS—THE BUSH, THE NAME

Exodus is filled with stories of dramatic proportion. One such story contains some of the most fundamental theology of biblical Israel as well as contemporary Judaism. It is the account of the burning bush and the revelation of God's name (Exod 3). It tells of the call of Moses and of his commission to lead the people out of Egyptian bondage. The tradition about the divinely appointed leadership of Moses is so deeply rooted in the faith of the people that they have handed it down in more than one version (cf. Exod 6). As we look at one of these versions, we can see its relationship with the other.

The Bush

There are elements in this story that connect it with another theophany (appearance of God), recorded in Exodus 19. The Hebrew for *"bush"* (*s'neh*) is thought to be an allusion to Sinai, the mountain where the covenant was made and where the law was given. The burning of the bush is linked to the fire on Sinai. These literary ties may be the author's way of connecting two traditions (the exodus from bondage and the revelation on the mountain) that were originally quite separate. The fact that the mountain is identified as Horeb (Exod 3:1) as well as Sinai (Exod 19:11) suggests that there is more than one tradition here.

Whatever the origin of the tradition might be, its meaning is clear. Moses is the recipient of a divine manifestation which legitimates him as a chosen instrument of God. It is through his leadership that God will deliver the people from the bondage of Egypt. It is through his mediation that God will give the Law.

The Name

In ancient Near Eastern thought, the name of the person was not merely an identification. It was also an intimate component of the very character of that person. One really only knew another when one was able to pronounce that person's name. To know and to be able to pronounce someone's name was to exercise a certain amount of power over that person. It is for this reason that many Jews neither speak nor write the personal name of the God of the Bible. Instead, they say "the LORD" or "my LORD" (the translation of *adonai*), and when writing they transcribe only the consonants (YHWH). At other times, they combine the vowels of *adonai* with the consonants YHWH. This yields the well-known title "Jehovah."

When Moses asked for God's name in order to convince the Israelites that God was indeed in relationship with them and that Moses had been commissioned by this God to lead them from bondage, God's reply was quite ambiguous: "I AM WHO I AM.

Tell the people, 'I AM has sent me to you' " (Exod 3:14). Here we have a play on the Hebrew words for "I AM" and the name YHWH. Scholars do not agree on the exact translation and meaning of the name. Many interpreters hold that the name itself is derived from some form of the Hebrew verb "to be." Some translate it, "I will be who I will be" or "I will cause to be what I will cause to be." All do agree, however, that every translation of it suggests that Israel believed its God was dynamically present to the people. This is because the Hebrews thought of "being" as something vibrant and active, not as the static "pure being" of Neo-Scholastic philosophy.

This name is different from other expressions used to speak of God, for example, "the God of Abraham, the God of Isaac, the God of Jacob" (Exod 3:6), "God Almighty" (Exod 6:3), "the Fear of Isaac" (Gen 31:42), or "the Mighty One of Jacob" (Ps 132:2). *They* merely describe some aspect of God. *This* name reveals something of the very being of God. It claims that to be YHWH means to be actively present to and involved with this people.

LEVITICUS—HOLINESS, CULT

Leviticus is a collection of rubrics and regulations governing the cultic life of biblical Israel. Its name is derived from the Levites, the religious leaders who served in various cultic capacities. The book itself does not tell a story, nor does it inspire as do the prophets. It deals almost exclusively with legislation. For this reason, too few people appreciate this book and the profound theology found within it.

Holiness

Holiness is the very essence of God. It is that mysterious quality of the divine that makes it "wholly other." The Hebrew word for holy (*qodēs*) means separate or cut off from, suggesting the distinct division between what is divine and what is not. The effect of holiness on human beings is twofold: because the deity is "wholly other," those who come into contact with God are terrified and repelled; because the fascination of the deity is overwhelming, they are attracted to God.

The holiness of God itself is inaccessible to us. All we can know about it is what God chooses to manifest. Even then, it is not really the holiness of God but rather the glory of God that is revealed, and this is usually revealed as power or righteousness. Since this holiness belongs to God, we cannot acquire it for ourselves through any effort on our part. Our only access to it is through some kind of contact which the deity alone can initiate. This contact makes one holy, set apart, and conscious of one's own powerlessness and moral unworthiness.

According to Leviticus, contact with divine holiness can be very dangerous, even fatal. This is why only those objects and those people who are holy, having become so by some special association with God, can presume to approach God. Even they must be protected from the power of divine holiness. One protection is consecration. Those who are not consecrated are denied immediate access to the holy. This also is to protect them from the mysterious power of the holy.

Cult

Israel believed that in a certain sense the entire nation was consecrated to God ("You shall be to me a kingdom of priests, a holy nation" [Exod 19:6]) and, therefore, every aspect of its life was circumscribed by laws regulating holiness. Most occurrences of the words *holy* or *holiness* are found in liturgical contexts. There the holiness of persons and objects is signified by a form of ritual consecration, after which they were considered ritually pure. Only what was holy, set apart, consecrated, ritually pure could be used in worship. What was not holy was regarded as profane. (Profane does not mean evil; it means religiously or sacrally neutral.)

The cult was the formalized way that people encountered God. It was usually enacted at designated places (shrines), at designated times (feasts), and by designated people (priests). If cultic worship was to be pleasing to God, it had to be carried out according to divinely approved requirements. The holiness of God had to be revered. The sacredness of the cult had to be assured. The purity of everyone and everything involved had to be guaranteed. Cultic legislation was formulated to accomplish these goals.

Israel had a rich and diversified cultic practice. The numerous festivals and the variety of functionaries involved in its celebrations gave rise to many rules and regulations which had one primary purpose: to enable Israel to stand in the presence of the holy God and worship God, and to survive that awesome power.

NUMBERS—WILDERNESS, MANNA

Everyone knows some of the stories found in the Book of Numbers, yet very few people actually read this book. Tribal censuses, lists of names, and a travel itinerary seldom excite or inspire. Still, the story of God drawing a people out of bondage and leading them to a land of their own would be incomplete without this very important segment.

Wilderness

The Hebrew name for this biblical book (*bĕmidbar*) can be translated "In the Wilderness." It was "in the wilderness" that the faith of the people was tested and found wanting. It was "in the wilderness" that they were disciplined and strengthened. Here wilderness should not be confused with some mystique of solitude or "flight from the world." Instead, the wilderness, terrifying yet purifying, was the way through which God led the people from Egypt to Canaan, from bondage to a land of promise. Only later in Israel's history was the wilderness perceived as an idealized place, and the period spent in the wilderness as a honeymoon (Hos 2:14-15).

While it is true that life in Egypt was difficult, life in the wilderness does not seem to have been much better. The people constantly complained about the lack of security (Num 14:2-3) and the scarcity of food and water (20:2-5). Life in slavery, difficult but assured, was preferred by some to what appeared to be the likelihood of death (14:4). The drudgery of Egypt seemed more tolerable than total dependence on God.

The inability of the people to put total trust in God may be difficult for us to understand. According to the story, they had only recently been miraculously released from Egypt. If God had performed such wonders then, why should they doubt God's care for them in the wilderness? Their complaints serve to underscore their own hard-heartedness and lack of trust and the triumph of divine patience and providence.

Time and again the people rebelled in the wilderness. Time and again God punished them. Each time, Moses intervened and God's anger was softened; the punishment was abated and the people were healed. In the final analysis, the period in the wilderness seems to have been less a time of Israel's faithlessness than of God's mercy.

Manna

The story in Numbers about the manna has a parallel in Exodus 16. There we read about the precarious situation in which the people found themselves, a situation that God remedied by daily providing this mysterious food. Unfamiliarity with this desert sustenance prompted the people to ask: *"Man-hu?* What is it?" (Exod 16:15).

In Exodus we read that God provided the manna in response to the murmuring of the hungry Israelites (16:7-8). In Numbers the people complain because "there is nothing at all but this manna to look at" (11:6). Clearly the wilderness tradition intends to show that God's providence was not a reward for the people's faithfulness. God's care for this discontented people was unconditional, and they did not appreciate it. In Numbers, they did not murmur out of need; they complained because of dissatisfaction.

Fresh manna was given on every day except the Sabbath. This not only shows that God was in the midst of the people even in that desolate place, but also that God was always *actively* present. This sign was so powerful that the people were commanded to preserve a container of manna in the ark of the covenant along with the tables of the Law. Thus future generations would be reminded of God's unconditional, active, provident presence in their midst.

DEUTERONOMY—COVENANT, LAW

We need not read far into the Book of Deuteronomy to discover the role played by the covenant. A brief look at this concept will help us to appreciate both the form and content of the book itself. We will then be better able to see the role that law played in the lives of the people.

Covenant

Simply stated, a covenant is a mutual pledge. It may be made between equals or between individuals or groups of different social standing. It presumes that no natural bond already exists. As understood in the ancient Near East, the covenant itself establishes a relationship similar to a blood bond. Covenant partners are bound to each other in a serious commitment, any violation of which incurs serious punishment.

Biblical Israel understood its relationship with God in terms of a covenant. While there is evidence that at times the covenant responsibilities rested heavily on God, it was usually Israel that was subject to various stipulations. Examples of the first type of covenant include the one made with Noah, where God promised never again to destroy the world by flood (Gen 9), and the one with David, where dynastic permanence was guaranteed (2 Sam 7). It is the second type of covenant, however, upon which the identity of the people rested. Entering into a covenant with God, Israel assumed the responsibility of a way of life that demonstrated its attachment to God and its commitment to societal harmony (Deut 5).

At first glance, it appears that the Book of Deuteronomy is a series of sermons given by Moses before the people entered Canaan, the Promised Land. Many scholars maintain that the sermons themselves are arranged according to the form of a covenant renewal ceremony. They contend that various traditions took shape within cultic celebrations and in the process took on the form of the celebration itself. Only later were these traditions reshaped into the form of sermons.

The content of the sermons is in fact reminiscent of the covenant renewal ceremony, which contains an instruction and exhortation, a brief history of God's goodness to the people, a list of stipulations by which the people are bound to God, a description of the actual covenant ceremony, and a list of the blessings that follow obedience and the curses that follow disobedience. It appears that the entire book is an elaboration of the covenant renewal ceremony.

Law

The Book of Deuteronomy, which means "second law," tells the story of Moses recounting the promulgation of the law that was given at Sinai. Those to whom this "second law" is given are the offspring of the people who left Egypt, encountered God at the mountain, and died in the wilderness having forfeited the chance to enter the land. The book itself is more than law in the strictest sense. It contains eloquent speeches that recall the past as well as promises that look to the future. Both the recounting of the past and the anticipation of the future focus on the gift of life in the land which the people are about to enter. The specific demands of the law are meant to enhance the new life that is opening up before them, a life to be lived in an exclusive relationship with God that overflows into the relationships between and among all the people.

Thus, law is not so much restrictive as it is descriptive and directive. It describes the special care that God has for the people, evident in the unique covenant that God initiated with their ancestors, and it directs them as to how they should live out that special covenant relationship. This relationship, which is one of steadfast love, is the foundation of law. Biblical law makes little sense outside of the context of the devoted covenant relationship.

JOSHUA—*SHOPHAR,* ARK, *HEREM*

The tenor of this book is clearly military. A closer look at the description of the destruction of Jericho, perhaps one of ancient Israel's best-known battles, suggests that frequently there is a layer of meaning here that is liturgical. This account of military conflict may contain, as well, elements of ritual reenactment.

Shophar

The *shophar,* often called a trumpet because it produced a clear, sharp sound, is the traditional ram's horn used to signal events of both war and peace. It warned of approaching danger in times of conflict (Judg 3:27), and it announced the liturgical celebrations of the new moon (Ps 81:3) and the beginning of the sabbatical year (Lev 25:9). It is still used in ritual settings to call Israel to worship.

The story of the battle of Jericho (Josh 6) repeatedly mentions the blast of the *shophar.* The ceremonial tone to this description leads us to believe that either the narrative is overlaid with elements of later liturgical celebrations of some actual victory, or the original event described here was in fact as liturgical as it was military. If the former is true, then the account is an example of the common religious practice of ceremonial reenactment of historical events, with elements from the reenactment becoming part of the original story. Insofar as the latter is true, we have a report of what has come to be called "holy war." (The meaning of "holy war" will be discussed under the Book of Judges.)

Ark

The ark served different functions throughout Israel's history. It acted as (1) a symbol of the presence of YHWH in the midst of the people (Num 10:33-36), (2) a war palladium affording effective protection from enemies (1 Sam 4:3), (3) an elaborate container within which was preserved a copy of the tablets of the Law (Exod 25:16), and (4) a portable throne upon which the invisible YHWH was somehow seated (2 Sam 6:2). Since the character of the account of the battle of Jericho is both liturgical and military, the ark's role within it is probably some combination of the four meanings mentioned above.

The liturgical elements of the narrative include the ceremonial procession with the ark of the covenant, the prominent role that the priests played in this procession, and the blowing of the *shophar* by the liturgical personnel and not by the military force. Still, the context of the narrative is one of warfare; the liturgical ceremony serves a military purpose. The author of this story apparently wished to depict the fall of Jericho as an act of "holy war."

Herem

Herem or "the ban" may be the most perplexing of ancient Israel's military practices. It called for the total destruction of everyone and everything belonging to the conquered enemy (6:17-26). The word *herem* is frequently translated "to devote," and is associated with the idea of holiness and exclusion. What was devoted to the LORD was banned from profane or private use. We find it difficult to imagine that YHWH would expect, much less demand, such a brutal practice. Whether Israel viewed the ban as a punishment of the enemies of YHWH, as a sign that this war had a sacrificial character and should not be personally profitable, or as a radical method of hygienic protection, the idea of *herem* still offends our sensibilities. Without denying the basic authenticity of the war narratives, commentators question the frequency and scope of the actual practice of the ban. It may not have been as unremitting and extensive as the narratives suggest.

JUDGES—WARS OF YHWH, INHERITANCE

The judges of the pre-monarchic period of ancient Israelite history are remembered more for their military exploits than for their legal expertise. With the exception of Deborah who was both a judicial arbiter and a leader in war (4:4-5), most are depicted as charismatic leaders who, when impelled by the spirit of the LORD, delivered Israel from its enemies. The majority of the conflicts between Israel and its neighbors resulted from territorial disputes. The claim that God had promised and was now giving the land to Israel lay at the heart of these conflicts (Josh 1:6).

Wars of YHWH

Sensitive readers of the Books of Joshua and Judges are often troubled by its frequent references to war and by its claim that military conquest was willed by God. The Bible does indeed relate accounts of tribal and national conflicts. It portrays YHWH—symbolized by the ark of the covenant—in the forefront of the armies, leading the people into battle. It also shows that the people acknowledged that the final victory belonged to

YHWH. Still, these wars probably did not have the significance that "holy war" has come to have. Today "holy war" ideology is frequently called upon to encourage people to enter into conflict. For ancient Israel, the concept "wars of YHWH" was probably a way of explaining and legitimating battles that had already taken place.

Certain features of this concept of "holy war" may have been a part of Israel's military strategy. Many accounts include blowing the *shophar,* a trumpet that signalled battle; the presence of the ark of the covenant, a religious symbol signifying YHWH's presence and protection; the practice of the ban, an injunction to assure that there would be no looting. It is clear that these military elements were also liturgical, whether in their original setting on the battlefield, or in their retelling during ritual reenactment, or both.

This designation, "wars of YHWH," was a way of expressing three important tenets of Israelite faith: (1) YHWH was the sovereign God, and in any battle would emerge victorious to establish order that had been threatened or disrupted and to ensure peace; (2) YHWH was personally present as protector and patron of the nation, leading it to security and prosperity; (3) those tribes and nations that threatened Israel were a threat to the God of Israel as well. In view of these tenets the people were assured that YHWH was their leader, that they were God's army, and that their wars were justified.

Inheritance

According to the stories found in Joshua and Judges, the occupation of the land of Canaan was accomplished through belligerent military campaigns. These were not wars of defense but of aggression. How could Israel possibly believe that it had a right to wrest land from people who were already occupying it? Without condoning the invasion, we should understand what probably contributed to Israel's attitude toward the land of Canaan.

A nomadic or seminomadic people like the ancestors of Israel are always in need of new grazing land. If they believed that their patron god was always looking out for their welfare, they would trust this god to provide whatever land they will need. Land was essential for their survival; God had provided in the past and would provide in the present and in the future; therefore, the land before them, land which they obviously needed, was God's gift to them. Even as they seized the land, they believed that it was God's land by right and their land by inheritance from God. This land had been promised to them by God for their use and for God's glory, and it was God's will that they take it.

RUTH—LEVIRATE, REDEEMER

The kinship laws of the ancient world were intended to safeguard not only the integrity of the clan but also its property. Two examples of kinship legislation are the law of levirate and the law of redemption.

Levirate

The law of levirate gets its name from the Latin *levir,* meaning "brother of the husband" (Deut 25:5-10). According to this law, if a man died without leaving an heir, one of his surviving brothers was required to take the widow as his own wife. The firstborn of that union was considered the child and legal heir of the deceased man. This practice accomplished three goals: (1) it guaranteed the survival of the deceased man's name, (2) it assured that his property remained within his clan, and (3) it made provision for the care of his widow.

The First Testament contains two examples of levirate marriage, the stories of Tamar (Gen 38) and of Ruth. Evidently, the earlier ancestral tradition (Tamar) was well known by the time of the writing of Ruth, for the author makes reference to Tamar and then traces the descendants of her son Perez through Obed, the son of Ruth, to King David (Ruth 4:12, 18-22). It should be noted that in these stories, both Tamar and Ruth had to resort to some form of trickery in order to get Judah and Boaz respectively to accept their levirate obligations. It seems that the biblical authors used this social custom to show that the promises of God, which were eventually fulfilled through David, would be thwarted neither by historical events (dying without issue) nor by human infidelity (reluctance to assume responsibilities).

Redeemer

Members of a clan had an obligation to help and to protect each other's person and interests. If, because of temporary financial setback, an Israelite had to be sold into slavery in order to pay debts, a near relative had the duty to redeem that person. If it was the inheritance that had to be sold in order to pay a debt, the relative had priority over all other potential purchasers. In this way the family property would not be lost.

The story of Ruth combines the custom of levirate marriage with the duty of redemption. When Naomi tells Ruth that Boaz is "one of our next of kin" (2:20), she uses the word *go'el* (redeemer). However, Boaz was neither a brother of Ruth's deceased husband nor the closest in kinship, and so the law of levirate did not apply in his case. If he was to act as *go'el,* the nearest of her deceased husband's kin first would have to relinquish his rights to the property about to be sold by Naomi (4:3). This is done in accordance with the laws of redemption (Lev 25:47-49). When this unnamed relative does relinquish his rights, the symbolic act of exchange which he performs (4:7-8) is suggestive of the ceremony associated with a man's refusal to comply to the obligations of levirate (Deut 25:9). In this one act the man disavows his levirate responsibility and relinquishes the property rights associated with it. Thus Boaz is permitted to step forward to claim the hand of Ruth, the widow of Mahlon, and to take charge of the inheritance of her deceased husband.

The interweaving of these two customs might reflect an actual historical development in Israel's law and practice. The fact that Elimelech's land did not revert to his closest male kin but was Naomi's to sell might show a development in property laws. On the other hand, the author of the Book of Ruth may have combined the levirate custom and the law of redemption for the purposes of this particular story. It becomes a way of incorporating the non-Israelite ancestress of David into the community. This book is an example of the concern within some circles in Israel for the questions of universality and inclusivity.

1/2 SAMUEL—PREDICTION, PROPHECY

It is a common misconception that the primary role of prophecy is the prediction of the future. It is clear that such an interest is present in several prophetic books, but by no means is this the essence of the prophetic movement. A brief look at some closely associated but clearly distinct concepts will provide a better appreciation of the office and message of the prophet.

Prediction—foretelling

Predicting the future appears to have been a part of the ministry of the prophets. If it is understood simply as the ability to tell the future in advance, it might be more correctly called divination. Divination attempts to predict the future either by interpreting signs and omens or by interpreting received oracles. A diviner works with some external object. This object is usually something in nature, or some arbitrary human action that is relatively common such as lots that have been cast, arrows shot into the air, the lines on the palm of the hand, birds in flight, or the entrails of sacrificial animals. Divination foretells the future by divining the meaning of these signs. This is not strictly prophecy as we have come to know it. Some prophets may very well have employed forms of divination, but the major religious prophets of Israel looked upon divination with disdain.

Closely associated with the diviner was the seer, who possessed the ability to comprehend what was not always accessible to all. The seer may have come to this special knowledge by means of divination, but this was not the only avenue. The term *seer* was the earliest designation of the prophet. Samuel is called both seer and prophet (1 Sam 9:9). Even with superhuman knowledge, the seer had no ecstatic experience but was like the diviner, a reader of signs and/or events, a foreteller of the future. The focus was not on the present.

Prophecy—forthtelling

Prophecy, on the other hand, is principally concerned with insight into some present situation. It contains an element of foretelling only to the extent that God's complete plan and total purpose will be realized in the future. When it does contain prediction, this usually looks to the immediate future, which impinges on the present.

The Hebrew word for *prophet, nabi,* can have both a passive and an active meaning. It designates both "one who has been called" and "one who calls." The former meaning focuses on the personal experience of the prophet, while the latter concentrates on the role that the prophet plays in the community. The word *prophet* itself comes from the Greek and means one who speaks for others—in this case, for God. The major prophets of Israel claimed to have been called by God to announce God's will. They maintained that their commission as well as their message came directly from God and, therefore, they felt compelled to speak. Some prophets experienced a kind of vision or possession by the spirit when the supernatural power contacted them (Amos 1:1; Isa 1:1; 6:1-8; Mic 1:1; Ezek 1). Nonetheless, the prophecy itself was intelligible and relevant, for it had to be received within the world of human beings.

The proclamation of the prophet was a forthtelling or speaking forth rather than a foretelling. The prophetic message spoke to the needs of the moment and was indispensable to the well-being of the community. Some prophets were active at the heart of the society, as significant members of the political or religious establishment. Others belonged to marginal groups and addressed the social scene from a less privileged position. The social context out of which, and the religious needs to which, the prophet spoke shaped the message that was delivered. Prophecy was always a response to a specific situation.

1/2 KINGS—PRINCE, KING

We can learn much about people by examining their ideas about leadership. Ancient Israel had several forms of leadership. Even within a single form—monarchy—we find different types and understandings.

Prince

In some of the narratives that tell us about the early monarchy, the ruler is called "prince" or "leader." (Although several Hebrew words are rendered "prince" or "leader" [e.g., *nagid, nasi, sar*], there is little difference in their meanings and they are often used interchangeably.) It may be that at the outset, Israel refrained from using the title *king* lest it succumb to the same idolatrous perversions that had corrupted its neighbors. Ancient kings often claimed divine characteristics and prerogatives. They envisioned themselves as direct descendants of the god or as divine manifestations in human form. The religion of Israel could not tolerate such arrogance from its rulers. They were not to view themselves as gods but as vice regents, responsible both to God and to the people. This may explain why, at the very beginning of their reigns, Saul (1 Sam 9:16) and David (1 Sam 13:14), as well as Jeroboam in the north (1 Kgs 14:7) were called "prince" or "leader."

The word *prince* was used in many different social situations. It refers to a person of exceptional power and authority. This leader might be chief of a tribe (Judg 5:15) or a warrior (1 Kgs 11:24). The elevated status was earned (charismatic) not inherited (dynastic). Biblical narratives clearly show that the people regarded an impressive military victory as testimony of God's favor. They may well have rallied around this warrior in hopes that he would lead them off of the battlefield as well. There is ample evidence that the extraordinary military leadership of some men made them likely candidates for royal administrative responsibility (1 Sam 9:16; 2 Sam 5:1-3; in both cases the word used is *prince*).

King

As the monarchy developed under the administration of David, the early fears about kingship either receded or were suppressed. The newly established royal rule seems to have been patterned after the governmental structures of surrounding nations. Perhaps David merely appropriated the bureaucracy of Jerusalem, the Jebusite city that he conquered. He not only established a successful monarchy, but a dynasty as well. The success of David prompted the people to believe that God had made a covenant with him and his descendants (2 Sam 7:11-16), and they placed their hope in this particular family. This contributed to making the monarchy a permanent institution, perceived as a vehicle of God's special favor.

The king had three main roles: (1) chief military leader of the nation, protecting the people from anyone or anything that would threaten their security; (2) supreme judge of the people, safeguarding justice within the nation itself; (3) officiating priest at cultic celebrations. The people believed that it was God's power that gave victory over external enemies, God's wisdom that safeguarded justice in the land, and God's glory that manifested itself during Israel's worship. They viewed the king as God's special agent of these blessings. This distinction was marked by the anointing that took place at the king's coronation, and it was at this time, they believed, that he was filled with the Spirit of God. The degree to which the distinction was revered is seen in the story of David. Although Saul sought to kill him, twice David refrained from utilizing his advantage over Saul precisely because he recognized that Saul was "the anointed of the LORD" (1 Sam 24:6, 10; 26:9, 11).

1/2 CHRONICLES—PRIESTS, LEVITES

The Books of Chronicles appear to be merely a retelling of the historical narrative found in the Books of Samuel and Kings. *Paraleipomena,* their name in the Septuagint (the Greek version), means "things omitted." This suggests that the books are simply an addition to the earlier story. Such an understanding misses the unique theological character of this material.

The Chroniclers were thoroughly committed to the religious traditions that had been handed down to them, but they were also mindful of the pressing needs of their own community, needs that were quite different from those first addressed by the stories describing the time of the monarchy. They realized that if the religious message of these traditions was to be effective within the existing community, it would have to be reinterpreted. Consequently, they retold the story of the past in ways that threw light on their present situation. They did this by stressing the liturgical institutions and practices of their own time, and by featuring individuals important to their community.

The significance of the Temple and its liturgy can be seen in the way the kings are portrayed. David is not depicted as the lustful, troubled monarch of earlier traditions. Instead he is the model king whose inspired prayer is preserved in the sacred songs. Solomon, whose extravagance and mismanagement contributed to the division of the kingdom after his death, is revered here as the one who built the Temple according to the command of God. Thus the history of the people is retold in a way that is attentive to elements of the earlier narrative, yet also new.

Priests

Israelite priests were attached to a shrine or temple where they served God through prayer and sacrifice and the community through mediation and teaching. The dignity and influence attached to this office frequently generated rivalry among the priests, as seen in some of the stories about Abiathar and Zadok, priests in the Davidic court (2 Sam 15:24-29; 1 Kgs 1:7-8). Eventually, the levitical priest Abiathar was expelled from the court of Solomon (1 Kgs 2:26-27). As the bureaucracy of the cult grew, the priestly duties were divided and the Levites lost more status. Although Levites served in the sanctuary, only an Aaronic priest could perform certain ceremonies such as mixing spiced ointments (1 Chr 9:30) and offering incense (2 Chr 26:17-18). And only a legitimate priest could become the prestigious high priest.

Levites

The Levites first appear at the time of Moses in the wilderness. There they represented the entire people of Israel and served as substitutes for the firstborn sons who belonged by right to God (Num 3:12). Their origin as priests is difficult to trace. One tradition states that they replaced Aaron after he had encouraged the people in idolatry (Exod 32:25-27). Another claims that they were chosen by Moses after the death of Aaron (Deut 10:6-9). A third states that they merely assisted the priest Aaron (Num 3:6).

Whatever the pre-Exilic traditions may suggest, the Chroniclers give Levites special prominence in the post-Exilic community. Their importance stems from their involvement and prestige in the highly structured liturgical practices of the day. Only the Levites were permitted to carry the ark of the covenant (1 Chr 15:2) and to minister before it (1 Chr 16:4). They had charge of the sanctuary, the sacred vessels, the preparation of the cereal offerings, and the service of praise (1 Chr 23:28-32). They were treasurers (1 Chr 26:20), musicians, and singers (1 Chr 16:4-7). They also assisted the priests as teachers (2 Chr 17:7-9), judges (2 Chr 19:8-11), even prophets (2 Chr 20:14-17).

EZRA/NEHEMIAH—SAMARITAN, PERSIAN

These books, considered a part of the work of the Chroniclers, show many literary similarities with the Books of Chronicles. Even more obvious are the theological concerns that they have in common. The city of Jerusalem, the cult, and the cult personnel all play the same significant roles in this literature. Insistence on separation from what is not purely Israelite marks this period and this theology.

Samaritan

Originally, the Samaritans were the inhabitants of Samaria, a city in the central range of ancient Israel. Built after Solomon's kingdom split in two, Samaria served as the capital of the northern kingdom of Israel (1 Kgs 16:23-33). Soon the entire region was known by this name (Hos 7:1; Amos 4:1). When the northern kingdom fell to Assyria in 722 B.C.E., a significant portion of the population was deported and foreigners were introduced into the land. From that time onward, the Samaritan people were viewed with contempt by the southern Judeans and their worship of YHWH was rejected as syncretism.

This history, along with the post-Exilic returnees' conviction that they alone were the true remnant responsible for the restoration of the nation, explains the passionate opposition of Ezra and Nehemiah to any Samaritan involvement in Israel's religious or political reconstruction. From their point of view, the northerners had always been unfaithful to the covenant that God had made with David and his household. After the Assyrian conquest, those with any Israelite ancestry who intermarried with the conquerors thereby relinquished their privileged position as children of Israel. Now that Ezra, Nehemiah, and the faithful returnees had been commissioned to rebuild the city and the nation, they would collaborate with no apostate. This antagonism between Jews and Samaritans forms the backdrop of several Second Testament scenes as well (Luke 9:52; 10:33ff.; John 4). To this day the Samaritans are separate from the Jews and have their own version of the Bible called the Samaritan Pentateuch.

Persian

The Babylonian Empire, which had put an end to the independence of Judah under the dynasty of David, had always faced a powerful rival, Media. This formidable empire had many vassal states, one of which was Persia. In about 550 B.C.E., the Persian king Cyrus rebelled against the Medes, captured their capital, Ecbatana, and went on to capture Babylon, the capitol of the Babylonian Empire.

Cyrus did not drive the conquered peoples from their homeland. In fact, he gave those in exile the opportunity to return to their native land if they so chose. He respected the local religions, allowing people to worship as their tradition dictated. He decreed that the Temple in Jerusalem be rebuilt at state expense (Ezra 6:3-5). Later Persian authorities supported Israel in the Temple reconstruction (Ezra 5:6–6:12). The impact on Israel of this change in the foreign policy of its conqueror accounts for the general characterization of Cyrus as both the "shepherd" and "anointed" of the LORD (Isa 44:28; 45:1).

As Israel returned to its own land to rebuild itself both politically and religiously, it was indebted to Persia for some of its political policies. Nonetheless, it remained hostile toward Persian religious influence. Suspicious of anything or anyone that could not trace its roots to the original pre-Exilic community of believers, Ezra ushered in an extensive reform. He denounced any marriages with foreigners that took place during the Exile. Appealing to marriage laws from an earlier time (Deut 7:3), he sought to reestablish Jewish identity by ensuring pure blood lines.

TOBIT—ANGELS, DEMONS

Traditional societies have always recognized the existence of powers beyond human control. Some of these powers seem benevolent and amicable, others malicious and threatening. Angels and demons play significant roles in several popular biblical stories. In fact, much of the drama in the Book of Tobit revolves around the influence exerted by the angel Raphael and the control of the demon Asmodeus.

Angels

The word *angel* means messenger in both Greek and Hebrew. The early biblical stories show that as intermediary beings between God and humankind they (1) communicate God's directives (Gen 22:11), (2) announce special events (Gen 16:11), and (3) protect the faithful and execute punishment on their enemies (Exod 14:19).

It is because they are in the service of God that angels are often referred to as "spirits." Characteristics common to Eastern mythology frequently appear in the descriptions of the angels themselves (e.g., wings) and of the service they perform. They make up the court of heaven (Isa 6:1ff.), support God's throne (Ps 80:2), draw God's chariot (Ezek 10:10), serve as God's mount (Ps 18:11), protect God's garden (Gen 3:24), and shelter the ark of the covenant (Exod 25:18f.). They usually appear in human form when they act as messengers, but even then they possess extraordinary knowledge and beauty.

Rarely are the biblical angels named. When they are, their names correspond to the roles that they play in a given situation. In the beginning of the story of Tobit, the angel calls himself Azariah (YHWH helps). At the end of the book, he identifies himself as "Raphael [God heals], one of the seven angels who enter and serve before the glory of the LORD" (12:15). Both names characterize the angelic role of mediator of divine activity on behalf of human beings. The angel is first a helpful companion and guide and later a healer.

Demons

Demons were originally thought to be personifications of lesser gods. It was only later that the term was used specifically for unfriendly divine beings. In this latter sense, the demon was seen as an enemy of human beings against whose power it was necessary to protect oneself. This protection was usually afforded by means of magic spells or incantations. It is this understanding that prevails in the Bible.

Although the early law codes of Israel prohibited the practice of magic (Exod 22:17; Lev 19:31; 20:27; Deut 18:10), such a prohibition does not appear to be in effect in this story. The young Tobiah is instructed by his angelic companion to burn the heart and liver of a fish in order to break the spell that the demon had over Sarah, his newly wedded bride. Repelled by the odor of the burning fish, Asmodeus flees (8:2-3) leaving Sarah free to enter into her married life without fear.

The name Asmodeus (3:8) is probably derived from the Hebrew word meaning "destroyer." However it is very close to the Persian Aesma Daeva, "spirit of anger." Since the setting of this book is the Persian city Ecbatana, the similarity is not coincidental. It may be that early Israelite belief in evil spirits was further developed by its contact with Zoroastrian religion during the period of Persian control. Since this book sets out to show that Jews can indeed remain faithful to their religious traditions even while living in the Diaspora (outside of the land of Israel), the triumph of an angel that stands at the throne of the God of Israel over a demon with Persian origins may have strong political overtones.

JUDITH—CANON, APOCRYPHA

One of the questions most frequently asked of the Bible by the average person is: Why do some versions have more books than others? This is not an insignificant question. While it may spring from a simple observation of disparity, it touches on the complexity of the formation of biblical tradition. All Christian

Bibles have the same Second Testament. It is in the First Testament that differences can be found.

Canon

A canon is an approved collection of biblical books. Believers hold that these writings had their origins in revelation and that they continue to be a source of revelation today. The word *canon* itself originally meant "reed," a stick that acts as a kind of norm for measuring. The biblical canon includes those books against which both our religious tradition and our lives are measured.

Ancient Israel preserved certain traditions as normative (acting as a norm or standard). Among these traditions were some whose importance was never questioned (Genesis, Exodus, Leviticus, Numbers, and Deuteronomy), as well as others not as widely accepted (Tobit, Judith, parts of Esther, and Maccabees).

The spread of Hellenistic thought and language in the third century B.C.E. prompted the translation of the Hebrew traditions into Greek. There were now two major versions of the Scriptures. Most of the subsequent biblical development took place in a Hellenistic context and so these traditions were preserved in Greek. It was not until after the destruction of the second Temple (70 C.E.) that the Pharisaic leaders of the Jewish community adopted the older and shorter Hebrew version as authoritative.

We are not sure why they included some writings and not others. At this time the Pharisees differed with some of the more apocalyptic-minded Jewish sects, and they may have taken a stand in favor of a more conservative interpretation. No doubt the choice was also influenced by the rivalry that had developed between the distinct Jewish and Christian interpretations, as well as the Christian practice of adding its own writings to the collection.

Christians did not close their canon of Jewish Scriptures until the second or third century. Even then it was not until the Council of Trent in the fifteenth century that the final decision was made. The Reformers rejected the authority of the papacy and its use of Scripture to authenticate some of its teachings. They looked to the Scriptures themselves as the norms for interpretation. In choosing the shorter Jewish canon as their official list, they have preserved the more ancient version. The Roman Church, in accepting the wider Greek canon, has preserved an authentic early Church tradition which includes some books not found in the Jewish canon.

Apocrypha

Apocrypha comes from the Greek word meaning "hidden." This suggests that the message of the apocryphal books was kept from the majority and understood only by the truly wise. Gradually the term took on a negative meaning because the orthodoxy of the books was frequently suspect. Today the term is used to refer to ancient Jewish and Christian books from the biblical period, or pretending to come from that period, that have not been accepted by the Church as canonical. Among these books are some called *pseudepigrapha* (false writing) because they falsely claim biblical authorship (e.g., The Assumption of Moses, The Secrets of Enoch). Protestants regard as apocryphal the seven books contained in the Greek version of the Scriptures but not in the Hebrew: Judith, Tobit, 1 and 2 Maccabees, Wisdom of Solomon, Sirach, and Baruch. Catholics call these books *deuterocanonical* (second collection of canonical books).

ESTHER—DIASPORA, PURIM

The Book of Esther is a tale of oppression and liberation. It tells of the threat of genocide, court intrigue, and the faith and courage of a woman. It is a story retold every year within the Jewish community, for it recounts their survival as a people. Forced to live outside of their own homeland, they were vulnerable to the whims of the citizens of the host country. Despite this, their religious faith and human ingenuity won the day.

Diaspora

Diaspora refers to the widespread settlement of Jews outside of Israel from the time of the Babylonian Exile through the Greek and Roman periods. While there probably were some Israelites who lived outside of the boundaries of the nation during every period of its history, the focus here is on a situation primarily caused by a resettlement that was forced rather than freely undertaken. *Diaspora* should not be confused with the dispersion of the inhabitants of the northern kingdom of Israel, who were deported and replaced by foreigners when that kingdom was overrun by the Assyrians in 722 B.C.E. Since we have not been able to trace the history of these people, they have come to be referred to by some as the "lost tribes of Israel."

The setting of the Book of Esther is the eastern Diaspora and the characters are observant Jews who not only live in Persia but who have prospered there. These Jews may have found it necessary to be somewhat assimilated into the dominant culture, but they did not really lose their Jewish identity. The heroine is a Jewish woman married to the Persian ruler, a situation that would have been severely condemned by Ezra and Nehemiah. However, the author of this book endorses dual allegiance: that is, allegiance to one's religious tradition as well as to the political system within which one lives.

Purim

The Book of Esther records the origin of a feast marking the repeal of the order to exterminate the Jews (9:20-32). The name of the feast, Purim, comes from the Babylonian word *puru,* meaning lot or destiny. In the story, the enemy Haman cast a lot to determine the day (13 Adar) for the extinction of the Jews (3:7; 9:27). Through the shrewd devices of an elderly Jew, this plot turned against him; the Jews were spared and Haman died in their place. 14 and 15 Adar were set aside to commemorate this reversal of destinies. The story highlights the superior wisdom of the faithful Jew over against the cunning of the Persian. The Diaspora did not undermine Jewish religious integrity.

Purim is not a religious feast like Passover. It has no cultic character and its observance is in the style of a carnival. It probably originated in Jewish communities of the eastern Diaspora. It is possible that the story does not recount an actual event but was created to explain an existing feast. The feast, however, may have been a commemoration of some sudden deliverance, the historical details of which were lost. The historical basis was reshaped by details of the festival, thus producing the legend of the feast.

Unlike other biblical stories, this book does not have characters that turn to God for help. In fact, in the Hebrew version of the book, the name of God is not even mentioned. Yet the fact that Jews would not compromise the heart of their Jewish identity gives this narrative an implicit religious character. Acting against Persian custom by approaching the king unannounced, Esther puts herself at risk in order to save her people. By identifying herself as one of the condemned she again places herself in mortal danger. It is this woman's loyalty to her heritage and her devotion to her compatriots that saves them, and herself.

1/2 MACCABEES—HASIDIM, HANUKKAH

The Hellenization of the ancient world created a new kind of religious challenge for the Jews. Many members of the upper class were enamored with elements of Greek culture and were open to the Hellenization of their way of life. Others who were zealous for the strict observance of the Law resisted any accommodation with Hellenism. This caused serious conflict within the Jewish community itself.

Hasidim

The term is related to the Hebrew *hesed* which means loyalty or faithfulness and refers to those people who opposed any kind of compromise with foreign culture. The Hasidim were committed to a definite Jewish style of life, one engendered by the Judaism they had inherited from their ancestors. They combined conservative religious loyalty with a nationalistic hope for the reestablishment of the Davidic kingdom. As Hellenism became more and more a threat to their beliefs, they developed into a kind of resistance movement. This resistance took two forms: armed conflict and martyrdom.

Jewish resistance was organized under the leadership of the priestly family of Mattathias (1 Macc 2:39f.). It took its name from his son and successor, Judas Maccabeus (1 Macc 2:66), a name that probably means "Judas the hammerer." A militant religious group participated in this revolt (1 Macc 2:42; 7:13; 2 Macc 14:6). (Some contemporary translations call them Hasideans, but the Hebrew word is *hasidim*.) These people may have been primarily concerned with religious liberty, but they fought for national independence as well. The later Pharisees and Essenes probably developed out of rival wings of this party.

Observant Jews, young and old alike, faced persecution (2 Macc 6:18–7:41). The elderly scribe Eleazar refused to save himself, believing that dead or alive he would not escape the hands of the Almighty if he defected (2 Macc 6:26). The moving story of a mother who was forced to watch her seven sons being tortured and killed only to be put to death herself shows the lengths to which faithful Jews were willing to go in order to uphold the Law.

Hanukkah

This minor festival, also known as the feast of Dedication (John 10:22) or the feast of Lights (the Jewish historian Josephus), is referred to as "the day of the purification of the temple" (2 Macc 2:16; 10:5). The name *Hanukkah* comes from the Hebrew word for "dedicate." In the year 167 B.C.E., Antiochus Epiphanes built a pagan altar over the Jewish altar of holocaust. Jews called this pagan altar the Abomination of Desolation (1 Macc 1:54; Dan 9:27; 11:31). Having victoriously recaptured the Temple site, Judas Maccabeus purified the sanctuary, built a new altar, and dedicated it on the third anniversary of its profanation.

This eight-day celebration is the only Jewish feast whose institution is connected with a traceable historical event, although recorded in a book that the Jewish community does not consider canonical. The Books of Maccabees may have been excluded from the Jewish canon because the Hasmoneans, the descendants of the Maccabees who became the ruling family from 142–63 B.C.E., proved to be unfaithful to the religious values cherished by those who shaped the Jewish canon. Second Maccabees explicitly relates this feast with the feast of Booths (1:9; 10:6). This may have been necessary in order to secure acceptance of the feast in parts of the Diaspora.

JOB—SUFFERING, SHEOL

The suffering of the innocent was a problem that troubled the people of the ancient Near East no less than it troubles us today. Since many people died before they seemed to have reaped the harvest of their lives, whether virtuous or wicked, God's justice was frequently questioned. One's fate after death was a different but related concern.

Suffering

Not all suffering is mysterious. If we are honest, we must admit that some troubles we bring on ourselves. At other times we are victims of the weakness or even the wickedness of others. Then there is the pain that accompanies diminishment, a fate that all living things must face. Finally, there are some situations of suffering that seem beyond our comprehension. The suffering of the innocent Job belongs to this last category.

The author goes to great lengths in the first two chapters to show that Job is not simply an honorable man, but even exemplary in his righteousness. It is clear that his affliction is not a punishment for sin. He is not really the object of the malice of other human beings, nor is his predicament merely a stage in the natural process of physical deterioration. The story tells us that Job's adversity is a trial (1:11; 2:5). As we read on, we discover that it is not really the afflictions in themselves that cause Job to agonize. It is the fact of not knowing *why* he is afflicted. He is convinced that he himself is not the source of his troubles and, not having eavesdropped on the council of God as did the readers (chaps. 1–2), he does not understand their origin or their purpose.

After arguing with those who insist that he accept the traditional explanations for suffering, explanations which he knows well but rejects as hollow, Job turns to God. He demands that God come to his defense, disclose the reason for his sufferings, and vindicate him. When God does respond, it is not with answers but with questions, questions that bring Job to acknowledge God's majesty and incomprehensibility and Job's own human limitations (42:2-6). Job comes to realize that there are situations in life that will always remain mysterious. In the face of them, all we can do is trust in the power and providence of the Creator.

Sheol

Sheol is often associated with "the pit," "the grave," "the land of darkness, dust, worms, and of no return," and thus, the underworld. It was probably observation of human decomposition that led people to believe that the dead no longer walked *on* the face of the earth; they were now *under* the earth. The origin of the word *Sheol* is uncertain. It may come from the Hebrew word meaning "to ask." This is quite plausible since the practice of necromancy (consulting the dead to discover the future) was quite prevalent in the ancient Near Eastern world.

Sheol was a place of neither reward nor punishment. Instead, it was a place of futile and meaningless existence for all the dead. The fact that ancient Israel even considered the possibility of an abode for the dead suggests its unwillingness to accept death as the absolute end of human existence. This attitude made possible the later theological development of the idea of a hopeful destiny for the dead. When Israel was influenced by astral religions and believed that union with astral deities in their heaven was the reward for fidelity, the underworld became a place of punishment.

Sheol is usually described as a place to be dreaded, but Job sees it as a refuge and an escape (14:13; 21:13). He regrets that in Sheol he will be unable to commune with God, but believes that at least there he will be beyond torment.

PSALMS—PSALTER, HALLELUIA

The Psalms have been known, loved, and used by religious people from the time of their origin to our own day. Even those who have little or no biblical knowledge recognize themes and phrases from the Psalms. They have been woven into the very fabric of the great literature of our civilization, and have been the inspiration of some of our most beautiful music. They continue to be the backbone of both our liturgical prayer and our personal devotion.

Psalter

The Psalter is another name for the Book of Psalms. It is really a collection of psalms that can be divided into five "books," perhaps in imitation of the Pentateuch (the first five books of the Bible). Each "book" ends with a doxology or declaration of praise of God (41:14; 72:18-19; 89:53; 106:48; 150:1-6). A close examination of the organization of the psalms reveals an even earlier stage of compilation in which there were at least three older "psalters."

The first of these older groups is called the "Yahwistic Psalter" or the "Psalms of David" (3-41) because the name YHWH is generally used and David's name appears in the title of most of these psalms. In the second, the "Elohistic Psalter" (42-89), the title *Elohim* (a plural form of "god") is used interchangeably with the name YHWH. Most of these psalms are attributed to David or to the Levite group known as the sons of Korah. The name YHWH is always used in the third collection, except in Psalms 108 and 144 which are composed of phrases from the Elohistic collection. Most of these psalms are credited to David.

Besides hymns of praise, the Psalms contain individual prayers of lament (e.g., 5; 51), of confidence (e.g., 23; 27), and of thanksgiving (e.g., 30; 40). There are also community prayers of lament (e.g., 94; 137), of confidence (e.g., 115; 129), and of thanksgiving (e.g., 65; 66), as well as royal psalms (e.g., 2; 110), wisdom psalms (e.g., 1; 37), and prophetic exhortations (e.g., 50; 81). The major events of Israel's history were remembered in the psalms, and there were appropriate psalms for every turning point in life.

Halleluia

There are several different types of psalms but all of them express some kind of religious sentiment. One of the best-known types is the hymn. This is a song of praise of God's goodness and majesty. It acclaims both the creative and the redemptive acts of God. The majority of hymns were probably composed for use during the liturgies of Israel's great feasts. They were set to musical accompaniment, and directives for this are still found within certain psalms (4:1; 5:1; 6:1). Various hymns also included an acclamation or a refrain, the most recurrent one being "halleluia."

This liturgical antiphon, which means "praise YHWH," serves as an opening invitation in some psalms (e.g., 111–13), a concluding exclamation in others (e.g., 104; 105), and both an initial invitation and a final response in still others (146–50). Some believe that "halleluia" is merely a liturgical addition, attached to the psalm to make it suitable for liturgy. Others believe that the psalm itself was designed around this acclamation of praise.

Several of these "halleluia" psalms (113–18) contain references to the Exodus and, for this reason, were sung during the yearly celebrations of Passover, Pentecost, and Tabernacles. They have come to be known as the "Egyptian Hallel," to distinguish them from the "Great Hallel" (120–36), which are processional psalms. A third group of "Hallel" psalms (146–50) acclaim God as the creator of the universe and the deliverer of Jerusalem. They may have been used during morning prayer. All of these psalms continue to be recited by Jews today, especially during these holy days.

PROVERBS—FEAR OF THE LORD, WAY OF WISDOM

This book is an anthology of instructions intended to provide a way of living that guarantees success and happiness. Its concerns are universal and perennial and its advice is very pragmatic. It is interested in prosperity and human fulfillment in this life, not in some future life. Because its focus is on human concerns, it might be called anthropology rather than theology. Still, since the ancient Israelites valued everything from a theocentric (God-centered) point of view, it might be best called theocentric anthropology.

Fear of the LORD

"The fear of the LORD is the beginning of wisdom." Several variations of this familiar saying appear in the Book of Proverbs (1:7; 9:10; 15:33). What does it mean? Are we to be afraid of God? Is not such an attitude behind the bothersome view of God as a stern judge or disciplinarian? Surely Israel had something more positive in mind. "Fear of the LORD" is based on the recognition of the holiness of God. This does not deny the presence of an element of terror in those who behold the awesomeness of

God and realize their own deficiency. Still, this idea is better characterized by awe and reverence than by terror and dread. Awe, not fear, is to be our response to the realization of God's activity in our lives.

The people of Israel learned some of the profound truths about life and the patterns of reality through simple but reflective observation. They saw the regularity in the heavens, in the environment, in ordinary social encounter. They believed that there was an inherent order in the universe which could be discerned and should be followed. They were convinced that happiness depended on being in harmony with this order. The wise person was the one who had discovered this order and was docile to it. The religious person believed that behind this order was an all-wise and all-powerful God.

To "fear the LORD" was to acknowledge and commit oneself to God revealed through this order. Knowledge about God was the beginning of true knowledge about the world. The more one was committed to God, the more one was in harmony with the orders placed in the world by this same God.

Way of Wisdom

How we understand "way" depends on how we understand "wisdom." Proverbs suggests that Israel perceived wisdom in three different ways: experiential, religious, and primordial. In each of these three perceptions, the "way" is the path that must be traveled if the desired goal is to be reached. Proverbs is filled with examples of the first kind of wisdom, advice gleaned from experience. The "way" of experiential wisdom is a course of action that is wise and prudent and leads to happiness (Prov 4:7).

We must never forget that ancient Israel's view of the world was fundamentally religious. Realizing that human wisdom is inadequate to insure lasting happiness, Israel believed that there is a dimension of wisdom that comes only from God. It taught that the "way" of this religious wisdom was the way of God, the way of religious fidelity (1:7).

Although the ancients struggled with many of the very questions that still trouble us, their understanding of reality was often quite different from ours. Therefore, the ways they answered some of these common questions may also be quite different. The third kind of wisdom, primordial wisdom, may be foreign to contemporary thought, but it was well known to the ancients. Primordial refers to the beginning of time, or even before the beginning of time, when creation took place through the wisdom of a god or goddess of creation. The "way" of primordial wisdom is the creative plan of the mediator of creation (8:22-31).

QOHELETH—VANITY

The Book of Qoheleth (or Ecclesiastes) may be one of the most underrated books of the Wisdom tradition, because it appears to have a negative attitude toward life. Qoheleth himself has been characterized as skeptical or cynical, even pessimistic. In reality, he may be more pragmatic than skeptical, more prophetic than cynical.

Vanity

"Vanity of vanities! All things are vanity!" Who of us has not heard that phrase? "You're so vain." The words of this popular song accuse the addressee of vanity. But, while the same word is used in both sayings, it does not mean the same thing. In the second statement, vanity implies excessive pride or attention to one's appearance. In the first, it indicates futility, emptiness, or worthlessness.

The Hebrew word for vanity means "to breathe, to exhale." It connotes something temporary and implies that trusting in something transitory is futile, generating only empty hope. It is from this point of view that Qoheleth comments on human striving after goals and human accomplishment of those goals. He has observed that many people never even have an opportunity to achieve the goals that they set for themselves or that are set for them. He, on the other hand, was fortunate enough to achieve his goals and partake of their fruits. However, his enjoyment was either empty or short-lived. He concludes that if the goals of success and happiness are beyond the reach of so many, or cannot satisfy people when they are achieved, they are worthless. Furthermore, it is futile to expect them to do what they cannot do, that is, provide happiness.

Like the rest of the Wisdom literature, the focus of this book is on the experience of life and the successful living of it. It is very concerned with what will guarantee the happiness that we all seek. The Wisdom tradition highlights some of the goals that promise this happiness. These goals, which cross cultural lines, have remained basically unchanged through the centuries. Women and men of all times and in all places have sought after health and long life, wealth and power, wisdom and the esteem of others. They believe that these things will bring the kind of satisfaction for which they yearn. It is to just such striving that Qoheleth speaks.

Health and long life are indeed goals that are worthy of our striving. How can we be happy and enjoy our success if we are bereft of life itself? But health and long life are so tenuous! To trust unreservedly in our precarious physical state is futile. The natural stages of diminishment complicate this even more. Health and long life cannot be trusted to secure our happiness. We should enjoy them if and when we can, but we must realize that our hold on them is tenuous and they guarantee nothing. To suppose otherwise is vanity!

The same is true of wealth and power. Some unforeseen mishap can snatch them from our grasp, and we can be left in a state worse than when we started. In the beginning of our striving we may have had some hope for achievement. Adversity can rob us not only of our wealth and power, but also of our hope.

Not even wisdom, that treasure held up by the sages as the prize *par excellence,* can guarantee happiness. This is especially true if we believe that wisdom itself should be rewarded. Life does not provide a surety of reward for anything. As for the esteem of others—this is probably the most fleeting of all. As easily as we can be held up by others, we can be cast down by them. Who knows what standards will determine respect and reverence? Even knowing such standards, we have no guarantee that they will not change overnight. To think that any of these things can assure one of success or happiness is vanity!

SONG OF SONGS—ALLEGORY, TYPOLOGY

The Song of Songs is a collection of poems celebrating nuptial and prenuptial love. Down through the centuries, both Jews and Christians have held that such erotic poetry should not be interpreted literally. Consequently, the book has been treated in several different ways. It has been viewed as an allegory of divine love, as a ritual reenactment of the dying and rising of a nature god, or as a drama depicting the courting of king Solomon and a country maiden. Only recently has it been regarded as a collection of love poems used at weddings. It is important to decide on the literary character of the Song, because that category will influence the way the book is interpreted.

Allegory

An allegory is a literary composition in which each detail signifies something outside of the composition itself. Of itself, it does not contain a factual or historically accurate account of events, but it points to some deeper spiritual truth. According to an allegorical approach to Scripture, the text really intends to say something other than what its literal meaning suggests. In reality, the deeper spiritual truth to which the allegory points is usually brought to the text by the readers, who read meanings into the images and actions that are derived from their own world view.

Traditionally, both Jews and Christians have explained the Song allegorically. The vividly portrayed sexual fantasies and encounters of the woman and the man have been seen as descriptions of the relationship of Israel with YHWH, the Church with Christ, or the individual soul with God. Thus, the explicit sexual imagery, which some people find difficult to reconcile with inspired religious ideas, can be understood symbolically as expressing profound religious sentiment. Although most contemporary scholars interpret the Song more critically, many people still prefer this more devotional approach.

Typology

Many people make no distinction between typology and allegory, but there is a clear difference. An allegory either denies or ignores the historical importance of a text and insists that it has a deeper spiritual meaning. Typology recognizes the importance of the historical elements within a text, but it also finds a clear link between these elements and other historically distinct or religiously significant persons, places, or events. It does not replace the original meaning. Instead, it adds another dimension to that meaning. According to this approach, the person, place, or event in the First Testament becomes a *type,* pointing to or foreshadowing a person, place, or event of the Second Testament. The latter is called the *antitype.* Only when the antitype appears does the full meaning of the type become apparent.

Typology is a way of dealing with the unity of the two testaments. It developed as a method of argument against those who failed to perceive Jesus as the fulfillment of Jewish expectation. It was also used against those who refused to admit that the First Testament was part of Christian revelation. Typology relates the testaments as promise is related to fulfillment, each being incomplete without the other. The danger of this kind of interpretation lies in its tendency to reduce the significance of the First Testament and the theology of Israel to a foreshadowing of the Second and a preparation for Christ.

Throughout the history of the interpretation of the Song, some commentators have rejected allegory's anti-historical perspective in favor of a typological interpretation. In their view, the passionate relationship portrayed may not necessarily be factual, but it is certainly true to life and it can serve as a type of human-divine love.

WISDOM OF SOLOMON—IMMORTALITY, THE FIGURE OF WISDOM

The Wisdom of Solomon (also known as the Book of Wisdom), though deuterocanonical (second-canon for Catholics, apocryphal for Protestants), contains some of the most highly regarded theology of the Wisdom tradition. It originated during the Hellenistic period of Israel's history when the learned of Jewish society were torn between loyalty to the traditions of their ancestral religion and acceptance of the cultural values of Greek civilization. The author of the book seeks to strengthen the religious commitment of the Jews by reinterpreting many traditional religious expressions and by showing that the new theology that emerges from this reinterpretation is both faithful to the tradition and relevant to the contemporary community.

Immortality

The Book of Wisdom says that "righteousness is immortal" (1:15) and that "hope is full of immortality" (3:4). This idea is also found in Psalms 112:3 and 119:142 where Israel praises the righteousness of the LORD that endures forever. Righteousness is a divine attribute. We share in it when we are in relationship with God. This notion of righteousness, much broader than a legalistic concept, suggests that our participation with God is somehow relational.

Israel held tenaciously to belief in its covenantal relationship. It was precisely such faith that led Israel to belief in immortality. If righteousness is a characteristic of God, and if covenantal fidelity meant union with God, then Israel could be called righteous as long as union with the righteous God lasted. Furthermore, if the righteous God is immortal, then this covenantal union could endure even through and beyond death. This is probably how Israel's notion of immortality evolved. Its use of Greek language and ideas enabled it to develop this notion in ways it was unable to do with an exclusively Hebraic mentality.

The Figure of Wisdom

A mysterious female figure appears in several of the Wisdom books. She is more than a wise woman; she is Wisdom itself. In the Book of Proverbs she is the one who addresses the readers, urging them to follow her instruction and inviting them to love her passionately (Prov 8:1-21; 9:1-18). In the Book of Wisdom, she is the object of Solomon's highest praise, described by him in language reminiscent of Isis, the Egyptian goddess of wisdom (Wis 7:7–10:21).

This representation of wisdom should not be considered as simply a figure of speech. While many passages maintain that one of the chief characteristics of God is divine wisdom, this representation suggests more. In addition to being a divine characteristic, here wisdom is itself some kind of personification of God. Wisdom Woman does what, in other places in the Bible, God does. She is "all-powerful, overseeing all," she "penetrates all things . . . can do all things" (7:23, 24, 27). We know that several other ancient religions venerated a goddess of wisdom (e.g., the Egyptian Isis and the Greek Athena). Although monotheistic Israel outlawed the worship of a deity other than YHWH, it did in some manner revere this elusive figure who today is referred to by some as the "feminine side of God."

Solomon's description of Wisdom is composed of elements from Israelite tradition (7:22a; see Prov 8:30), from the cult of the Egyptian deity Isis (goddess of wisdom and patron of culture whose praises were extolled in the form of lists similar to that found in 7:22–8:1), and from Hellenistic philosophy and science (see 8:7 for mention of the cardinal virtues of Plato). This description may be the heart of the author's argument for the superiority of the wisdom of Israel.

SIRACH—SEPTUAGINT, ECCLESIASTICUS

The Book of Sirach is known by several different names. Translating the title of the Greek version we have Sirach, Wisdom of Sirach, or Ben Sira (the name of the author). The Latin name, Ecclesiasticus, may be more familiar to Roman Catholics. The canonical status of the book is disputed by some, and so it belongs to the collection called deuterocanonical (second-canon) by Catholics and apocryphal by Protestants. In the foreword to the work, the grandson of Ben Sira states that he translated the teachings of his grandfather from the original Hebrew (a version lost to us) to Greek, and edited this translation to the form that has come down to us, in order to show the Jews of his day that real wisdom was to be found in the traditions of Israel and not in Greek philosophy.

Septuagint

Septuagint is the name applied to the oldest Greek version of the First Testament. It means "seventy" (and hence is sometimes abbreviated LXX), which alludes to a tradition claiming that, just as seventy elders accompanied Moses up the mountain when he received the Law (Exod 24:1, 9), so seventy elders were responsible for translating the Hebrew Torah into Greek. This tradition is based on the contents of a letter written by a certain Aristeas. The letter alleges that there were actually seventy-two elders, six from each of the twelve tribes, working independent of each other and yet able to produce the same (thus obviously inspired) translation of the Bible.

This work was probably done in Alexandria sometime during the third century B.C.E. There was a large Jewish community there at the time, and the Greek used in the book is of the type associated with that city. The Septuagint is not only a translation. It is an interpretation as well. Many ideas and images that originated from a Jewish perspective were reshaped and significantly changed in the process. The Septuagint stands as an example of the Hellenization of Israel.

Ecclesiasticus

The book is called Ecclesiasticus, from the Latin meaning "church book." It probably got this name because it was used so often as a catechetical aid in the early Church. The Christian theologians Cyprian (third century C.E.) and Jerome (fourth century C.E.) attest to such use. Clement of Alexandria (second century C.E.) quotes it so often that his citations have come to be considered an authoritative version of the text. The early Christians seem to have preferred the Alexandrian Bible, and so it is not surprising that the influence of Sirach can be detected in some of their writings. The Letter of James is an example of this. Both books address questions of pride (Sir 10:7; Jas 4:6), and humility (Sir 3:18; Jas 1:9), of rich and poor (Sir 10:19-24; Jas 2:1-6), and of true wisdom (Sir 19:17-21; Jas 3:13-17). There are obvious parallels between directives found in Sirach and those found in the Gospels. This includes teachings on magnanimity (Sir 29:12; Matt 6:19) and forgiveness (Sir 28:2; Mark 11:25) and against placing false hope in possessions (Sir 11:18-19; Luke 12:16-21). In Sirach we see personified Wisdom searching for a place to dwell and finally pitching her tent in Jerusalem (24:1-12). Traces of this poetic characterization can be found in the Prologue to the Gospel of John where the Word, present with God from the beginning and involved in the creation of all things, "pitched his tent among us" (John 1:1-14).

This controversial book continues to exercise its influence even today. Though it is less known than are Proverbs or Job, more passages from it are included in the Roman Lectionary than from any other Wisdom book. In this way, the teachings of Ben Sira continue to exhort hearers to fidelity to the tradition and to upright moral living.

ISAIAH—MESSIAH, SERVANT OF THE LORD

The message of this book addresses historical situations that span from the second half of the eighth well into the fifth century B.C.E. However, its importance lies not only in its historical specificity but also in its ongoing relevance. Vague allusions to a godly figure who will come in the near future to inaugurate the righteous reign of God have been cherished by believers since the time the tradition first developed. The image that these allusions project and the promise that they contain have inspired people in their longing and have sustained them in their wait.

Messiah

The title *Messiah* could refer to anyone who was chosen by God to realize the destiny of Israel. The word itself is derived from the Hebrew for "anoint." The Messiah was "the anointed one." Since kings, prophets, and priests were among those anointed at different times in Israel's history, messianic figures were envisioned as being royal, prophetic, and often cultic leaders. Among these characterizations, the most prominent is the royal messiah.

In spite of the promises of God and their royal privileges, the kings were often unfaithful both to the covenant and to their administrative responsibilities. Still, the people believed that God is faithful and they trusted that the promises that God had made would be fulfilled through the instrumentality of some future king. This message of hope was at the heart of the teaching of some of the prophets, especially Isaiah (Isa 9:2-7; 11:1-9). He instructed Israel to look forward to the time when an "anointed one" would be true to his call to be leader and would be the vehicle of God's special favor for the people.

This royal messianism developed in various and equally rich directions in the post-Exilic theology of Israel (Zech 6:11-12). Although the fall of the Davidic dynasty caused the prophets to look elsewhere for hope, the royal character of this future leader was never completely erased.

Servant of the LORD

A second figure, distinct from but in later religious thought often associated with the royal messiah, is the Servant of the LORD. Mention of this servant is found in four Isaian passages referred to as "Servant Songs" (42:1-4; 49:1-6; 50:4-9; 52:13-53:12). Although these four separate passages are quite similar in tone and content, they do not form a single unit. They are not only independent of their respective contexts, but also independent of each other. Yet, together they have generated a portrait of a pious agent of God's compassionate care.

The identity of the servant that emerges from this composite has always been a mystery. Is it an individual (49:1) or is it the entire people (49:3)? Is the mission of the servant to Israel itself (49:5) or to the nations (42:1)? One thing is quite clear: the servant will have to suffer (50:6), and this suffering will be in the place of others (53:4-6) and for their deliverance (53:10).

The servant appears to behave as both king and prophet. First, and perhaps most importantly, he is endowed with the spirit of God (42:1). Like a king he establishes justice (42:1, 3-4), and like a prophet his ministry is a ministry of the word (49:2; 50:4). However, this is no ordinary king or prophet. This is an innocent man whose anguish seems itself to be his principal service. His mission is not primarily to effect the transformation of others through his judging or his teaching; rather, through his suffering he himself becomes the reparation for their sin.

JEREMIAH—ORACLE, CONFESSIONS

This book is a collection of utterances of Jeremiah reflecting events of Judah's history during the reign of its last four kings, and of biographical information that reveals something of the character of the prophet himself. Although the poetry and prose of the book tend to be gathered into distinct sections, there is no consistent narrative, nor is there a clear organization of literary forms. However, a brief look at two of these forms will offer a way of entering into the message and emotion of the book.

Oracle

Prophetic speech is "messenger speech" and the basic prophetic form is the oracle or pronouncement, either of judgment or of salvation. Since prophecy is regarded as the word of God, it is frequently framed in divine first person and introduced by phrases such as "thus says the LORD" (Jer 2:5; 14:15; 22:3; 34:2; 47:2; 51:58), or "the word of the LORD came to me (or him, or Jeremiah)" (Jer 21:1; 13:3; 28:12; 39:15; 42:7). In oracles of judgment, the judgment itself is either preceded or followed by the indictment which lays bare the sin for which sentence is passed.

It seems that the reform inaugurated by Josiah (c. 628–609 B.C.E., 2 Kgs 22:1–23:25), which Jeremiah no doubt wholeheartedly supported, did not take root in the nation, and after the king's death the people returned to idolatry (2 Kgs 23:26-37). Thus Jeremiah proclaimed judgment against both Judah (13:1-27) and its neighbors (12:14-17), against both the citizens of Jerusalem (11:1-5) and the reigning king (21:11-24).

Although Jeremiah employed the typical formula of prophetic oracle, he was unique in the way he used it. He frequently prefaced his accusation with a kind of rhetorical question which set the stage for his indictment ("Can the Ethiopian change his skin? the leopard his spots?" [13:23]). The pattern is but one of the literary characteristics of Jeremiah's speech that has led scholars to conclude that although this prophet ministered in the southern kingdom of Judah, he had more in common with the northern prophetic tradition. This may have resulted either from his early commitment to Josiah's reform, which was inspired by the northern covenant theology found in the Book of Deuteronomy, or from a post-Exilic editing of his oracles in light of Deuteronomic theology.

Confessions

Another group of oracles (11:18–12:6; 15:10-21; 17:14-18; 18:18-23; 20:7-18) contain Jeremiah's complaints against his personal enemies and also against God. No doubt other prophets faced opposition and desolation, but no comparable complaints have been attributed to them. These "confessions" depict the prophet in great anguish, mocked by others, facing failure, and experiencing abandonment by God. These complaints share many of the characteristics of the psalms of lament and were most likely derived in great part from this source. Still, the confessions probably expose the profound inner struggles of this tragic man. Not only were his hopes dashed by the ill-fated death of Josiah, but he had to deal with Judah's national blindness, knowing that disaster was imminent.

Most of the "confessions" are really prayers to God (in three of them the LORD appears to reply [11:21-23; 12:5-6; 15:19-21]). There we discover a man who was by nature sensitive, introspective, and reluctant to assume the role of "prophet of doom." Not only had he been chosen for a mission that seemed opposed to his natural disposition, but he was denied the support one might hope for from a marriage companion (16:1-13). His solitary life itself proclaimed the devastation and isolation that infidelity was to wreak on the nation. Despite this suffering, Jeremiah could still take delight in the word of the LORD (15:16).

LAMENTATIONS—DIRGE, LAMENT

The Book of Lamentations consists of five tightly structured poems describing the destruction of Jerusalem. Each poem has an acrostic structure, wherein the verses in some way follow the sequence of the twenty-two character Hebrew alphabet. Many verses of the book are written in a *qînâ* form, where the first half of the sentence consists of three strong beats and the second half, of two. This imbalance produces a kind of falling rhythm that resembles a choke or a sob. The literary structure itself conveys the notion of lament. It is from the translation of *qînâ* (lamentation) that the book gets its name in Greek, Latin, and English.

Dirge

The best example of a funeral dirge is found in the description of David's lament over the deaths of Saul and his son Jonathan (2 Sam 1:17-27). There the form is both explicitly identified as a *qînâ* and preceded by the characteristic dirge expression "ah, how!" (*'êkâ*). (In Hebrew manuscripts, the Book of Lamentations derives its name, "Ah, How!," from this word.) Chapters 1, 2, and 4 of Lamentations all begin with this opening word and, although the literary style changes throughout the chapters, parts of these poems can still be regarded as a form of a funeral dirge. As with actual funeral dirges, these poems recall the former beauty of the city even as they describe its present desolation.

The use of the dirge enabled Israel to mourn the defeat of the people, the destruction of Jerusalem, and the devastation of the land in the same way as one would mourn the death of a loved one. This is not surprising, for what was dearer to the Israelite than Jerusalem? It represented the people and was the place chosen by God as the site of the Temple, God's special dwelling place on earth. The loss of the city was synonymous with the demise of the nation. In the first dirge (1:1-11), the desolation of the city is bemoaned. In the second (2:1-12), the severity of YHWH's punishment is deplored. The third dirge (4:1-16) is similar in theme and content to chapter 2 where Jerusalem's humiliation is contrasted with its former splendor.

Lament

The book contains both individual and communal laments. The material of chapter 3 exemplifies the first type, while chapter 5 is an example of the second. In neither case, however, is the complaint in its purest literary form. Chapter 3 is a collection of first person singular laments (3:1-18) followed by an expression of trust (vv. 20-24). Each verse designates some form of suffering as punishment from God. Here, the depiction of the bereft woman of chapters 1 and 2 gives way to a male speaker. The identity of this speaker is not clear. This may not have been a problem when the poem was recited during worship, because then the one reciting the poem took on the character of the one uttering the lament. However, in written form, the identity of the speaker is ambiguous; yet this ambiguity serves to draw the reader into the anguish being expressed.

The communal lament of chapter 5 is quite different from the other poems of the book. It is not an acrostic; it does not have the *qînâ* meter; and the sentiments are not those of an individual but of the entire community. The poem is not a complaint about the nation's misfortune but a prayer addressed directly to YHWH, begging for divine compassion despite the indisputable infidelity of the people. The humiliation of Jerusalem (v. 18) and the defenselessness of its inhabitants (vv. 3, 11) are recounted in admission of Israel's guilt and in an attempt to lay its distress before YHWH. The lament closes with a hymn acknowledging God's greatness and with a plea that God will restore the nation to the covenant relationship that it enjoyed in earlier times.

BARUCH—AUTHORSHIP, JERUSALEM

The alleged author of the book is Baruch (1:1-4), Jeremiah's companion and secretary. Characteristics of the text itself lead us to conclude that such ascription of authorship is a literary fiction. First, the historical information with which the book begins (1:1-14) is inaccurate. Second, analysis of the material suggests that this is more a collection of material originating from different times and different authors than it is a unitary composition. It may have been attributed to Baruch because, other than Jeremiah, he was the only individual who is believed to have witnessed the destruction of Jerusalem in 587 B.C.E. and left behind written records describing it (Jer 36).

Authorship

The composite character of the book attests to various influences. The prayer of the exiles with its historical introduction (1:1-3:8) bears striking resemblance to the prayer of Daniel (Dan 9:4-19), which grew out of the Maccabean crisis (167 B.C.E.). The hymn in praise of wisdom (3:9-4:4) is written in the style of Hebrew Wisdom literature (Bar 3:9—Prov 4:20; Bar 3:15—Job 28), while the poem of consolation (4:5-5:9) is reminiscent of the post-

Exilic prophet Deutero-Isaiah (Bar 4:5, 27, 30—Isa 40:1). The final section of this poem was probably inspired by Psalms of Solomon XI, a non-canonical collection of psalms compiled during the middle of the first century B.C.E. (Although it is really a separate work, the Letter of Jeremiah is sometimes considered the sixth chapter of the Book of Baruch.)

In the ancient world the religious character and canonical value of a book was often decided on grounds of authorship. Books that could claim Mosaic or prophetic or Solomonic authority were revered as sacred and their message was believed to be revealed. There are several different ways in which a book might acquire such distinction. (1) It could have been either written by the actual author or dictated to a scribe. The early oracles of Jeremiah (1–25) are considered by most as examples of this type. (2) It could have come from a disciple who was able faithfully to represent the thoughts of the author. The prose narratives in the Book of Jeremiah are thought to be compositions of Baruch (26–45). (3) It could have been written in the theological tradition of a well-known author. Attributing the entire Law to Moses and the Wisdom writing to Solomon exemplify this kind of authorship.

Jerusalem

The name *Jerusalem* means "foundation of peace." This Jebusite stronghold was already very old when David captured it and made it the capitol of his new empire (1 Sam 5:6-8). *El Elyon,* the high god of heaven and ruler of the earth, was worshipped here (Gen 14:18-24). Scholars believe that elements from this pre-Israelite theology were taken over and transformed by the Yahwist faith. As a result, the city continued to be revered as the holy mountain upon which God dwelt (Ps 48:2-4) and from which God ruled (Ps 93:2). This city had been especially chosen as the place of God's presence among the people (Ps 132:13). The building of the Temple served to establish the city as the permanent abode of God (1 Kgs 8:27-30; 9:1-3). Thus Jerusalem became a symbol of the constant saving power of God (Ps 125).

It is no wonder that the fate of this city played such an important role in the history and theology of the people. With the destruction of the Temple and the loss of the city came Israel's questions about the continued presence of God in their midst. We see this in the consoling poem at the end of Baruch. There the widowed and childless city itself cries out in distress (4:9-29), and is comforted with a promise of restoration (4:30-5:9).

EZEKIEL—VISION, SYMBOLIC ACTION

"The heavens opened and I saw divine visions" (Ezek 1:1). This phrase characterizes the prophetic experiences of Ezekiel. Visions that are difficult to understand and actions that to us seem bizarre comprise a significant portion of this book, and the prophet himself emerges from these pages as an extraordinarily complex individual.

Vision

Visionary experience does not seem to hold the importance in the early prophets that it does in later ones. In the former, the emphasis is more on the message that issues from the supernatural experience. The later prophets record unusual phenomena more extensively. The inaugural vision of Ezekiel, like that of Isaiah (Isa 6), was undoubtedly a profound, transforming experience. While its description may be symbolic, its meaning was probably not as foreign to the ears of the original audience as it is to us. The fact that the word for vision found in Ezekiel comes from the same Hebrew root as does the word for seer—which denotes "prophet"—points to the intrinsic relationship between the seer and that which was seen. The vision was a vehicle for the word of the prophet.

Was Ezekiel's experience really as bizarre as its description would lead us to believe? This is a difficult question to answer. Mystical experience of any kind transcends what is commonplace, thus rendering customary description inadequate. Prophetic vision, ecstatic in nature, is usually recounted in rather elaborate imagery. This imagery reveals more about the prophet's perception of the phenomena and of the historical conditions to which he must address his message than it does of the divine reality itself. The Exile was a time of great social, political, and religious upheaval. Hence, any encounter with the divine demanded a reversal of attitudes and behavior. Most likely, this message had to be delivered in words and acts that would startle the people and evoke a docile response.

Symbolic action

The Hebrew word meaning "to speak" appears in contexts where the word clearly indicates action. The realism of Semitic thought is evident here. The dynamic power that was released through speech flowed into action. This resulted in a merging of the prophetic word with prophetic action.

The force of the visionary experience of the prophets compelled them to proclaim the message of God in both word and deed. We find dramatization of such messages throughout prophetic history. Ahijah tore his garment into twelve pieces, thus symbolizing the division of the kingdom of Solomon (1 Kgs 11:30-32). Isaiah walked in captives' garb proclaiming Assyria's subjection of Judah (Isa 20:2). Chapters 4 and 5 of Ezekiel contain descriptions of symbolic acts relating to the siege of Jerusalem and the Exile. The first act (4:1-3) is clearly a staging of the siege of the city. The second act (4:4-8) symbolizes the burden of guilt that the people must bear. The third (4:9-17) characterizes the hardships that the siege will bring. And the fourth (5:1-4) demonstrates several different fates that await the inhabitants.

The passion of Ezekiel heightened the intensity of his dramatizations. The eccentricity of his behavior came from both the awesomeness of his encounter with the living God and the urgency of the message that he was commissioned to proclaim. We may not understand the nature of Ezekiel's encounter with God, but its effects were as dramatic as they were all-encompassing. The force of this experience transported the prophet to distant places, captured his imagination, and catapulted him into a religious eccentricity that continues to baffle even as it inspires.

DANIEL—KOSHER, APOCALYPTIC

The book gets its name, not from its author, but from the hero of the story. The theological character of its contents has been classified in different ways. In the first section (chaps. 1–6), Daniel is described as a wise man, an interpreter of dreams, and an exemplary foreign member of the court, much like Joseph in Egypt (Gen 37–50). Such a portrayal has its roots in the Wisdom tradition. For this reason, in the Hebrew Scriptures the book is found in the third part of the canon, among the other Writings. The Greek-speaking Jews, from whom came the Septuagint, regarded Daniel as a prophet and placed the book along with the other prophetic writings. This latter canonical grouping is generally used by Christian communities.

Kosher

One of the major concerns of the Book of Daniel deals with the extent to which a devout Jew can assimilate into a foreign culture. The first narrative in chapter 1 addresses this question. Daniel and his companions refuse to eat the food offered at the king's table and request a kosher diet, one in keeping with their religious observance. *Kosher* comes from the Hebrew word meaning "fit, proper, or acceptable." Kosher food is food that is by law acceptable, and was probably so judged because it conformed to customary categories.

There were no dietary restrictions on the fruits of the land. From the beginning, they had all been given as food (Gen 1:2). However, dietary laws did regulate the selection and preparation of animals, birds, and fish. For instance, only animals that both chewed a cud and had cloven hoofs were fit to eat (Lev 11:26; Deut 14:3-8). Birds of prey were forbidden (Lev 11:13-19; Deut 14:12-18), and fish had to have both fins and scales (Lev 11:9-12; Deut 14:9f.). Meat and milk were not to be mixed (Deut 14:21), and the consumption of blood was forbidden (Lev 7:26; 17:10-17).

The complexity of these laws makes clear why observant Jews would refrain from eating food prepared by foreigners. The dates of these law codes suggest that they were in force after the Exile rather than before. There is further biblical evidence of Diaspora Jews faithfully carrying out dietary requirements that gave them a distinctive identity (Jdt 12:1-4; Tob 1:10f.; 1 Macc 1:62f.).

Apocalyptic

Apocalypse comes from the Greek word meaning "revelation." It is a kind of religious thought that envisions two distinct and opposing ages, one evil and the other good, the forces of which are in conflict with each other. This kind of thought often appears during times of great social, political, or religious upheaval. It pictures the death of the present evil age and the birth of another. The historical and cosmic forces of good and evil are in mortal battle, and good is about to triumph. While the focus of this world view seems to be on devastation, its message is really one of assurance that out of the prevailing misery a "new age" will emerge.

The apocalyptic message is visionary in form and character (Dan 7). Knowledge hidden from the beginning of time is revealed to some venerated person by a heavenly mediator. Because this literature grows out of political turmoil and personal danger, the identity of the recipient is usually concealed beneath a pseudonym. Ancient prophecies are scrutinized in search of explanations for the present turmoil. At the heart of apocalyptic hope is the belief that something is about to happen that will shake the earth at its foundations and be cosmic in scope. The mixture of historical and cosmic elements produces imagery that is both bizarre and majestic. Such imagery and pseudonymity enable this protest literature to survive undetected in the midst of persecution.

HOSEA—JEZREEL, *LO-AMMI, LO-RUḤAMA*

There are few biblical passages that express the tenderness of God's love better than Hosea 2:21: "I will espouse you to me forever; I will espouse you in right and in justice; in love and in mercy." The verse reflects the covenant theme that is so much a part of the message of this prophet. It highlights the initiative that God shows in establishing and then reestablishing a relationship of love with the people. Some of the imagery that Hosea employs in expressing this covenant theology is suggestive of intimate familial bonds that are formed, threatened—even destroyed— and then reforged. The symbolic names given to his children are

examples of this. They describe both the intimacy of the covenant relationship and the alienation that resulted from Israel's sin.

Jezreel

The meaning of this name is more politico-geographic than
covenantal. It designated the site of a bloodbath that had taken
place at the defeat of the house of Ahab and the establishment
of the dynasty to which the reigning king, Jeroboam II, belonged
(cf. 2 Kgs 9:15-37). This name served as a warning of the fate
that would befall Israel (Hos 2:24). Considered geographically,
the natural fertility of the valley of Jezreel made it the breadbasket
of the country. For this reason, this name was also a symbol of
fresh and abundant life, certainly a covenant promise.

Lo-Ammi (Not-my-people)

Israel prided itself on being the "people of God." Tradition
shows that this way of thinking and speaking was used from earliest times. It was a way of referring to the unique covenant made
between Yahweh and the people, characterized by the technical
phrase, "You are my people; I am your God." It is very important to remember this when considering the implications of the
name of Hosea's second son.

At the time of Hosea, the sins of the northern kingdom had
become so grievous and so persistent that God, through the
prophet, disowned the people and placed this child before them
as a constant reminder of their alienation. The people had totally
and consistently violated their covenant pledge and so God ter-
minated the relationship and declared that "you are not my people
(*lo-ammi*), and I am not your God" (1:9).

Lo-ruḥama (Not-pitied)

The name of Hosea's third child is derived from the Hebrew
word for "womb." Pity, compassion, and mercy, also deriva-
tives of this word, all refer to the attitude one has toward a child
of one's womb or toward those born of the same womb. It implies familial relationship and demands commitment toward and

concern for one another, attitudes present within a loving covenantal relationship.

The name *Lo-ruhama,* like *Lo-ammi,* signifies God's rejection of the people. Israel's continued disdain of its covenantal responsibility destroyed the relationship and God cried out, "I no longer feel pity for the house of Israel; rather, I abhor them utterly" (1:6). Once these had been God's people and God had been compassionate toward them. Now their own sins had changed all this and the names of Hosea's children were a constant reminder of the people's new status.

Despite the tragedy of Hosea's own family life and the infidelity of the people of Israel, neither situation ends on this disastrous note. There is hope for restoration and rededication: "I will have pity on *Lo-ruhama.* I will say to *Lo-ammi,* 'You are my people,' and he shall say, 'My God' " (2:25). This hope is also expressed in 2:3: "Say to your brothers, *'Ammi,'* and to your sisters, *'Ruhama.' "* The message of the prophet reveals that the compassionate God cannot remain alienated from this people.

JOEL—NATURE, PENANCE

There is considerable debate about the interpretation of this book. Some think that it reflects a Temple liturgy conducted in hope of relief from the locust plague that is described within its pages. For others, the recurring mention of the Day of the LORD suggests an apocalyptic influence. Still other interpreters regard the plague as the onset of the Day of the LORD, a time of judgment for both Judah and its enemies.

Nature

The drama of this book moves from a report of an actual plague to an account of an invading army, to reference to the Day of the LORD. This has led to various interpretations of the nature of the locusts. The most obvious explanation is that this was a natural disaster, characterized as an invading army and understood to be the direct consequence of the sins of the nation. Others regard the locusts as apocalyptic harbingers of cosmic doom rather than as real creatures of natural disaster. Regardless of how we interpret the plague, the relationship between punishment for sin and natural disaster is quite plain. The character of human behavior somehow affects the rest of the natural world.

Today many people maintain that environmental disasters are often the result of human abuse of natural resources. They contend that these crises are simply the natural consequences of human disregard of the laws that govern a particular ecosystem. In this anthropocentric (human-centered) point of view, humankind is considered the active subject and the rest of creation is seen as an object. Another view is gaining acceptance today. It insists on the integrity of all of creation and contends that humankind, as unique as it may be, is but one active member of the cosmic system. Because of the harmonious interaction between and interdependence among all members of this system, the behavior of one member affects the entire system. This latter position is closer to the biblical view than is the former.

In the ancient Near Eastern world view, all of creation was governed by the same or similar laws. There was a moral dimension to the natural order and morality was determined by a natural law. Consequently, discord of any kind upset the balance of all things. This explains why people sought a moral explanation for natural disaster.

Penance

Many Christians recognize the call to penance in 2:12-17 as part of the liturgy of Ash Wednesday. Fasting and weeping and mourning (2:12; 1:9, 13f.) were typical expressions of repentance, but here Joel is calling for more than external gestures ("Rend your hearts" [2:13]). Furthermore, this repentance was not to be merely a manifestation of individual piety. Since the locust plague attacked the entire nation, the entire nation must have been culpable. Therefore, all of Judah was called to penance ("Blow the trumpet in Zion!" [2:15]). This period of repentance extended even to those individuals usually exempt from penance, such as children and newlyweds (2:16).

A scientific world view might question whether fasting can alleviate a plague. This matter would never have been questioned by the early Israelites, who perceived everything as interrelated and interdependent. If human sin could upset the order of nature, repentance could correct it. While Israel believed that this world order came from God and was upheld by God, it believed neither that the world merely follows some mechanical design beyond God's control, nor that God is constrained by any created order. God is free. That is why Israel made supplication, in the hope that God will be "gracious and merciful" (2:13).

AMOS—SOCIAL JUSTICE, WOE

At the very heart of biblical religion is the conviction that faith does not transport us into the transcendent domain of the gods. Instead, God's personal revelation takes place in *our* world and during *our* time. This conviction can be very consoling on the one hand and fill us with fear and trepidation on the other. It all depends upon the character and quality of our relationship with God.

Social Justice

Israel identified itself as a people in covenant with God. This relationship was a communal reality and included community obligations. In fact, the quality of Israel's relationship with God was measured by the character of its life as a community. Covenant partners were considered as close as family members and they were to be treated with the same respect and concern. It seems that at the time of Amos, socioeconomic differences had created a kind of class system in northern Israel that was an affront to covenant solidarity. Wealthy landowners took advantage of their positions and not only neglected the less fortunate within the community, but actually oppressed them. Judges were dishonest (5:7), merchants and landowners were unscrupulous (5:11-12). Even worship had been perverted (4:4-5). In straightforward and scathing words, Amos denounced this violation of covenant responsibility (2:7; 4:1; 5:11; 8:4-6).

Amos' condemnation of this social situation argues that in disregarding the social obligations of covenant election, Israel had also forfeited any claim to covenant privilege among the nations. Israel could no more make claim upon God's indulgence than could the Ethiopians, the Philistines, or the Arameans (9:7). Amos rejected, as false security, any notion that covenantal affiliation guaranteed divine protection regardless of the quality of covenant commitment.

Woe

A woe is a form of prophetic judgment-speech. Like other judgment-speeches, it contains an accusation of transgression and an announcement of the punishment that is to come. It differs from other judgment-speeches in its introductory exclamation— "Woe!"—which is itself an announcement of distress. The woe is associated with lament for the dead (1 Kgs 13:30). Sometimes it is contrasted to blessings, in which case it functions like a curse (Isa 3:10-11; Luke 6:20-26). Woes are usually found in series or in groups of two or three, as is the case in Amos (5:18-27; 6:1-14).

These woes accuse Israel of false hope and false security and announce some resulting affliction. The first woe follows a lament over the death of the nation, a specter which must have startled those people whose good fortune had blinded them to their inner corruption. In the face of the people's presumption that the advent of God would bring them even more good fortune, the prophet cried out: "Woe to those who yearn for the day of the LORD!" (5:18a). Neither their liturgical observance nor their sacrificial compliance would guarantee any exemption from the demanding justice of God (vv. 21-26). To think otherwise was to labor under false hopes.

The second woe denounces the nation's haughty reliance on prosperity and military strength. Amos challenged this people, who believed that they were impregnable: "Woe to the complacent in Zion, to the overconfident on the mount of Samaria" (6:1a). Their affluence (vv. 4-6), their strongholds (v. 8), and their victories (v. 13) had inspired a false sense of security.

Since the woe is not only a form of confrontation but also an expression of grief, as he denounces the crimes of the nation, the prophet also mourns the impending doom of the people he loves.

NAHUM/OBADIAH—JUDGMENT

Both of these short biblical books illustrate Israel's belief in God's moral judgment of the nations, executed through the agency of historical events. The Book of Nahum is a collection of proclamations of delight over the fall of Nineveh in 612 B.C.E. This city was the capital of Assyria, the nation that had destroyed the northern kingdom of Israel in 722 B.C.E. (2 Kgs 18:9-12). The Book of Obadiah, the shortest of all the First Testament books, is a vicious denunciation of Edom, a nation that enjoyed ethnic ties with Israel but was nonetheless its adversary.

Judgment

Israel believed that YHWH was the "Lord of history," in control of events and sovereign over all people. They also maintained that YHWH was a just god, who rewarded righteous behavior and punished transgressions. As a consequence, they regarded national calamity as a form of divine judgment. Several prophets characterized the Exile as deserved judgment for the nation's faithlessness. At times, they even viewed the conquering nation as the instrument of God's judgment on Israel. Such a message, as harsh as it may sound, points the accusing finger inwardly at Israel.

From earliest times divine judgment was also perceived as directed against the national rivals of Israel (Judg 3:9f.; Isa 13-27). Since Israel was God's chosen people their enemies were viewed as God's enemies. They believed that God would intervene in judgment against these other nations, and this judgment would be fully manifested on Israel's behalf on the Day of the LORD (Amos 1:3-5). A vindictive nationalism is found in later material. There we find psalms of cursing and imprecation (Pss 83; 129) as well as books like Nahum and Obadiah. Thus Israel believed that God used other nations to punish their enemies. Events of both their past and their future were interpreted in terms of divine intervention of judgment in their favor.

The annals of the kings of Assyria are replete with accounts of their plundering the treasures of the nations they had conquered. The prophet Isaiah records the tribute that King Hezekiah was forced to pay the Assyrian king Sennacherib for the safe deliverance of Jerusalem (Isa 36). For almost two hundred years,

Assyria had overrun the ancient Near Eastern world, subduing and plundering its neighbors far and near. Although the Book of Nahum has been criticized for its unmitigated enjoyment of the misfortune of Nineveh, the city that came to symbolize Assyrian oppression, it is no wonder that the prophet took delight in its demise.

According to the biblical story, the animosity between Israel and Edom can be traced back to the womb of Rebekah where Jacob and Esau, the progenitors of the nations Israel and Edom, first struggled with each other (Gen 25:22-26). This enmity was reignited when, on its entrance into Canaan, Israel was refused passage through Edom (Num 20:14-21). Many interpreters believe that Edom even collaborated with Babylon in its conquest of Judah and destruction of Jerusalem in 536 B.C.E. (Ps 137:7).

Neither Nineveh nor Edom was destroyed simply because it overran an innocent Israel. On the contrary, the people of God had sinned and, from their own religious point of view, deserved their subsequent downfall (722 B.C.E. in the case of Israel and 536 B.C.E. in the case of Judah). The condemnation of those other nations stemmed from their having taken unjustified advantage of the people during the times of their greatest vulnerability. Both the defeat of Nineveh by the Babylonians and the prophetic condemnation of Edom were seen as divine recompense for the treachery with which they had dealt with God's people.

MICAH/JONAH—UNIVERSALISM

An important element in Israel's identity, an element found in other ancient Near Eastern religions as well, is the conviction that it had been chosen by God to be a special people. Many of their laws and customs and much of their liturgical practice attest to this sense of separateness. The character of Israel's interaction with other nations reflects this fundamental notion. They believed that what was not Israelite was "unclean" and was to be eliminated or avoided. Much of their fierce military conduct was an attempt to cleanse the land of whatever and whoever was unclean, while their practices of separation and exclusion were ways of avoiding what they could not remove. Yet despite the centrality of this notion of election, we find an element of universalism running through Israel's national story from its very first chapter ("All the communities of the earth shall find blessing in you" [Gen 12:3]) to its last (Cyrus the Persian commissions the rebuilding of the Temple [2 Chr 36:23]).

Universalism

In a section believed by many to have been added after the Exile, Micah portrays Jerusalem as the center of divine instruction to which will come all the nations of the earth (4:1-5; cf. Isa 2:2-4). This hope for the restoration of Israel, coupled with the inclusion of other nations, exemplifies the optimism of some during the late Exilic period, optimism both for national restoration and for some form of universal understanding. This particular passage has been interpreted in several different ways. Some believe that the nations' coming to the mountain of the LORD implies their acceptance of the Law (4:2) and, therefore, the faith of Israel. Others contend that the "way" and "path" of the LORD (4:2) are themes from the Wisdom tradition, a tradition that is not as ethnocentric as is the national story. They argue that the nations will come to Israel for wisdom, not for the Law, and they believe that 4:5 corroborates this interpretation ("For all the people walk, each in the way of *its* God" [emphasis added]). Whether it is Law or wisdom that is sought from Israel, the passage represents a definite universalistic attitude.

The whimsical nature of the story of Jonah veils the cutting edge of its message. The Exile brought into bold relief the bitterness and vengefulness that some in Israel felt toward those nations that had oppressed and conquered it. Nineveh, the capital of ancient Assyria and the city to which Jonah was sent, epitomized for Israel the "evil empire." This was the city at whose hands God's people had suffered a great deal of misery and disgrace. This was the city whose defeat was celebrated by the prophet Nahum. This was the city whose sins against God's people had placed it beyond the realm of God's salvation.

The story is a kind of parable that challenges the narrow nationalistic world-view of some of those in Israel. The prophet Jonah is a caricature of the author's self-righteous compatriots.

When he is charged to go to the people of Nineveh and mediate to them the message of God's retribution, he not only flees from his mission but he makes himself ridiculous in the process. The twist in the story comes when the Ninevites hear and accept the prophet's call to repentance and, as a consequence, God relents and forgives them. It was because he knew that God is "gracious and merciful" and might save the Ninevites from doom that Jonah tried to escape to Tarshish in the first place (4:2). Now that his worst fear had been realized and the people had indeed repented, Jonah would rather die than accept the universality of God's compassion (4:3). The moral of this parable is clear. Israel is being told that such narrow nationalism disavows the universality that plays such an important role in their tradition, from the ancient ancestral story onward.

HABAKKUK—THEODICY

Within the prophetic literature, Habakkuk is unique in both form and content. Unlike other prophetic books, its central ideas are not expressed in the typical "messenger speech." Instead, it consists of a kind of dialogue between the prophet and God, wherein the prophet complains about the dire circumstances that the nation is enduring, and God responds. The content is neither consolation nor warning as is the case in most prophetic oracles. Rather, divine management of the world is challenged by Habakkuk and then defended by God.

Like other prophets of his time, Habakkuk struggled with the impending Babylonian threat. However, his message was less concerned with the immediate dangers that faced the people or the consequent misfortune that they would endure, than with a more fundamental problem: Why did God allow such a catastrophe in the first place? The issue was not merely retribution, that is, belief that the good would be rewarded and the evil punished. Retribution, whether we accept its claims or not, is a way of explaining the *source* of suffering. Habakkuk acknowledged the infidelity of the nation and the justice of its punishment (2:4-19), but he complained because the circumstances of the national disaster seemed unfair. The innocent suffered along with the guilty; some sinners seemed to escape hardship; and all of this was at the hands of the enemies of God. How could God have allowed chastisement to happen in this way? The theological issue with which Habakkuk grappled was theodicy, the problem of whether God really rules the world with justice.

Theodicy

Underlying the question of theodicy are two fundamental presuppositions. The first is the sovereignty of God. Biblical faith claims that God is omnipotent and that this omnipotence is absolute and exclusive. God, and only God, is all-powerful. The second presupposition concerns God's righteousness. It was out of goodness that God created in the first place, and everything that God created was good. Herein lies the dilemma: If God is righteous, from what or whom does evil originate? And if this righteous God is all-powerful, why does evil persist? The theory of retribution at times provides a partial answer. Evil originates from sinners, and suffering is the just recompense for sin, meted out by a righteous God. However, retribution as an answer falls short in the face of the suffering of the innocent. In such circumstances, either the power of God or the righteousness of God is challenged. Both Job and Habakkuk are examples of this kind of challenge.

Habakkuk's initial cry, "How long, O LORD?" (1:2), is commonplace to those who have seen anguish and injustice, but can do little or nothing about it, and who wonder why God is silent in the midst of such misery. Like Job, Habakkuk directs his complaints heavenward. Unlike Job, he receives at least some kind of an explanation. However, the words he hears offer neither comfort nor assurance. They speak more from the point of view of retribution than from that of mercy and forgiveness.

However, a word of hope comes obliquely, reminiscent of the divine response in other places in the Bible. The prophet is told that "the just shall live by faith" (2:4). The "just" are those who have been faithful to the covenantal relationship. The word for "faith" denotes steadfastness, confidence, trust. It suggests that the just will continue to trust God in the midst of, indeed despite, adversity. This declaration is the heart of the message of Habakkuk. As with Job, there is no answer to the "why" of suffering, but there is an example of "how to" suffer.

ZEPHANIAH—DAY OF THE LORD

The very earliest traditions of Israel suggest that the people believed that their God had chosen them from among all the nations, had directed them in all of their wanderings and in all of their dealings, and cared for them through every period of their history. Set apart from all other peoples, they experienced divine intervention as salvation. Hence their confusion and dismay when their own prophets announced that God would indeed come to them, but not to save them. Instead, God would come to judge them and to punish them for their infidelity.

Relatively little is known about the prophet Zephaniah, but elements of his message have played prominent roles in later Jewish and Christian traditions. For example, it is Zephaniah who elaborated the theme of the Day of the LORD as a day of woe for Israel as well as for the nations, a concept that first appeared in Amos. It is Zephaniah's description of this Day of Judgment (1:14-18) that was translated into Latin as *Dies Irae* (day of wrath) and became the theme of the sequence for the Catholic Mass for the Dead. In addition, the theme of the remnant of Israel, a people humble and lowly (3:12-13), is found in this prophetic book.

The Day of the LORD

The concept of the Day of the LORD is both rich and complex. Many hold that it originally referred to a time of military victory. Ancient Israel believed that God would defend the people from other nations and that this would be accomplished through some magnificent display of divine power and might. It would be a day of light for the Israelites, but one of gloom and darkness for the forces opposing them. They presumed that God would execute justice in the form of salvation for Israel and judgment for its enemies (Isa 13), since the enemies of God's people were surely the enemies of God as well. Initially, Israel believed that this divine victory would take place in history. However, the battle and its ultimate success took on an eschatological character as the prophets gave it cosmic significance (Isa 24:21-23).

The cosmic characterization of the Day of the LORD incorporated elements of a creation myth, which recounted the primordial battle between the forces of two competing gods. One of the gods was the embodiment of order and the other was a comparable embodiment of chaos. In the myth, chaos was conquered and its forces were restrained (see Ps 74:12-17). A combination of the military theme and the cosmic motif is found in Psalm 24. It shows that the central theme of Israel's liturgical celebration was the victory of God over historical and/or cosmic enemies.

All of this characterization comes together in Zephaniah's description of the impending wrathful Day of the LORD, a day that will strike dread in the hearts of all. Descriptions of both political and cosmic upheaval, natural catastrophes, and the horrors of war of any kind rush in upon one another in this portrayal of comprehensive and profound devastation.

As appalling as is the description of this Day of the LORD, it was intended to lead the people to repentance and transformation so that they might rejoice once again (3:14). This utterly bleak picture of the future does contain glimmers of hope. For "on that day you need not be ashamed of all your deeds, your rebellious actions against me" (3:11). Also, a remnant will survive the horror of this dark and terrible day, a people humble and lowly (3:12; 2:3). For these few faithful, the Day of the LORD will be a day of salvation, just as the earliest traditions had believed it would be.

HAGGAI/ZECHARIAH—RESTORATION, MESSIANIC AGE

Shortly after the Persian king Cyrus defeated Babylon, he issued an edict which allowed all exiled people to return to their homelands. He also provided for the return of sacred vessels that had been taken from the Temple in Jerusalem and for funds toward the rebuilding of that Temple (Ezra 1:1-4). Some, though not all, of the exiled Israelites saw this as an act of salvation by their God and they began to prepare themselves for the journey back to Israel. The excitement and anticipation of this homecoming that we find in Second Isaiah (52:1-12) quickly turned to the disillusionment and despondency found in Third Isaiah (58:1-7). Restoration of the social, political, and religious life of the people was not an easy feat to accomplish.

Into this scene stepped Haggai and Zechariah, two prophets intent on the restoration of Israel. Both men insisted on the rebuilding of the Temple and the reinstitution of the proper cult, as well as the reestablishment of an independent Israel. The first task was accomplished around 515 B.C.E. The second would have to wait until the Maccabean revolt of 167 B.C.E.

Restoration

It appears that the returnees were not met with a warm welcome. Their efforts to rebuild the Temple and the city walls were thwarted by the people already in the land, some of whom had remained behind during the Exile, as well as by the inhabitants of the old northern kingdom of Samaria. As a result, very little construction was completed between the laying of the foundation (c. 538) to 520, the year that King Zerubbabel and Joshua the priest arrived from Babylon. In the latter year both Haggai and Zechariah warned that God would no longer stand for delays. The Temple had to be built or the people would suffer the consequences of their negligence.

Haggai claimed that the drought and agricultural disaster the people were enduring was an instance of divine judgment (Hag 1:2-11). It seems that this oracle so moved the king that the work of restoration was started immediately. When the work began to lag, the prophet promised a Temple of such grandeur as to eclipse the Temple of Solomon. He may have been unable to keep this promise, but it did accomplish what he had hoped: work was resumed. Zechariah shared Haggai's passion for rebuilding the Temple and purifying the community. In eight symbolic visions, he encouraged the returned exiles, especially the leaders Zerubbabel and Joshua. Being from a priestly family, he gave special emphasis to the role of the high priest (Zech 3).

Messianic Age

The oracles of these prophets suggest that the hopes for a rebirth of an independent Israel centered on the Davidic king Zerubbabel (Hag 2:20-23; Zech 3:8; 6:9-14; see Isaiah 9 and 11). It was hoped that this royal descendant would restore the house of David to its former glory and would fulfill the ancient ideal of kingship.

He was regarded as the servant of the LORD (Hag 2:23; Zech 3:8), God's signet ring (Hag 2:23) which would give validity to all decisions.

The royal messianism of these prophets, especially Zechariah, had special significance for the earliest Christians. Many Second Testament writers described the life and works of Jesus with images borrowed from the latter half of the Book of Zechariah. There we find a reference to sheep with no shepherd (Zech 10:2; see Matt 9:36; Mark 6:34) and to a shepherd's wages of thirty pieces of silver (11:12; see Matt 26:15; 27:3-10). Finally, the accounts of Jesus' triumphal entry into Jerusalem reflect Zechariah's description of the arrival of the victorious messiah, a humble man of peace (Matt 21:1-9; Mark 11:1-10; Luke 19:28-38; John 12:14-15).

MALACHI—"MY MESSENGER"

We do not know who wrote this book, because "Malachi" is not a proper name. It comes from the Hebrew word meaning "my messenger" (see 3:1), and refers to the one through whom this particular message was given. The anonymity of the prophet may stem from the contentiousness of the times. The institution of oral prophecy seems to have been rapidly falling into disrepute (Zech 13:2-5). Not only was the prophet at risk, a fate faced by many prophets in the past, but prophecy itself had become suspect. To claim "Thus says the LORD!" may have carried little weight. Therefore, a question-answer exchange through the mediation of one referred to merely as "my messenger," might have been the best way to announce God's message.

"My Messenger"

The book is in the form of a dialogue between God and the priests in company with the people. Through the messenger, God makes an assertion (1:2a) to which the priest or the people respond with a question that challenges God's assertion (1:2b). Next the divine word is explained (1:3-4) and the exchange ends with a strong form of divine statement (1:5).

In the period following the prophesying of Haggai and Zechariah and the subsequent rebuilding of the Temple, religious fervor apparently began to wane, and the effects of laxity could be seen everywhere. For example, intermarriage was allowed (2:11), divorce was uncomplicated (2:14), and the vulnerable of society were oppressed (3:5).

Malachi stands in the strong prophetic tradition that condemns injustice and cultic carelessness. He denounced many of the abuses that Ezra would later work to abolish. He is also one of a long line of prophets critical of the incompetency of the priesthood. The role of the priests was primarily that of teacher. According to the covenant with Levi, they were responsible for proclaiming true doctrine (2:1-9). The priests were to function as "the messenger of the LORD of hosts" (2:7). Because they were remiss in this office and did not teach the commandments of the LORD, this mysterious Malachi seems to have assumed the role of messenger.

The final chapter of the book announces the arrival of God in judgment. Malachi's description is unique in that the LORD's appearance will be preceded by the advent of a messenger who will purify the Temple cult and the priesthood (3:3-4). Whether this purifying messenger will be the same as the earlier messenger of the covenant is unclear. Most commentators maintain that this latter messenger was really a herald from the divine assembly who was responsible for preparing the people for the advent of God. A later editor appended the announcement of the return of Elijah before the great and terrible day of the LORD (3:23). This does not mean that it was Elijah who would purify the cult and the priesthood. Rather, he would heal the family, the foundation of the Jewish community. The return of Elijah is significant since there is an early tradition that recounts his ascension into heaven (2 Kgs 2:1-11), but not his return. As a result, a later tradition arose predicting both his eventual return and the role that he would play on the day of fulfillment in the rejuvenation of the family and the reestablishment of the tribes of Israel.

This addendum may have complicated the original prophetic message, but it continued as an important aspect of Jewish eschatology which maintained that Elijah would reappear. Some of Jesus' contemporaries thought that he was Elijah returned

(Matt 16:14; Luke 9:8). Although John the Baptist seems to have rejected such an understanding of himself (John 1:21), the later Christian community saw him as fulfilling the role of Elijah (Matt 11:14; Mark 9:12-13; Luke 1:17).

MATTHEW—REIGN OF GOD, REIGN OF HEAVEN

One phrase that appears quite frequently in the Gospels is "reign of God." Although this is the form more frequently found, the author of Matthew's Gospel seems to prefer "reign of heaven." These expressions, while interchangeable, are not identical. Nor are they synonymous with "Church," a term common to the Epistles but found only twice in Matthew.

Reign of God

Although this expression is itself rare in Jewish literature, it has very old and treasured roots in the tradition of biblical Israel. It signifies the actual sovereignty or rule of God rather than the territorial sphere or realm within which God rules. From the beginning it had both political and religious significance. In the earliest period of Israel's history, YHWH was regarded as the people's exclusive king. (This fact played an important role in some of the initial opposition to the monarchy; see 1 Sam 8:7-9.) Initially, Israel believed that their God's sovereignty was exercised only over them. Other nations had their own divine kings. Gradually, the teaching of the prophets brought new insights into the nature and scope of God's rule.

The religious upheaval of the Babylonian Exile prompted Israel to spiritualize the concept of God's rule. As it came to realize that the establishment of this ideal reign would be the work of God rather than that of a merely human ruler, it began to anticipate a kingdom of the future, a reign that would be truly God's. Its boundaries would be determined neither by territorial considerations nor by any concrete sphere of power. This reign of God would be established in history, but in a way not limited to the usual geographic or political boundaries. Its presence would be characterized by righteousness and love.

There was also a temporal dimension to the reign. Israel looked for a future that would fulfill every hope. The prophetic writings contain several poetic descriptions of this ideal time (e.g., Isaiah 11-12). Before the reign could be brought to final completion, all of the enemies of God and of Israel would have to be conquered. This cosmic battle, which is described in Daniel 7, would take place both in and beyond time. The ultimate fulfillment of this hope might be realized outside of history, but its beginnings are within history. As Jesus proclaimed: "The reign of God is already in your midst" (Luke 17:21).

Reign of Heaven

It seems that later Judaism developed an awe and reverence for the name of God. The title LORD was substituted wherever the name YHWH appeared. In many places the sacred name was completely avoided and the word *heavens* was used instead. Perhaps a sensitivity to this concern of the pious Jews who became members of the Christian community explains Matthew's preference for the phrase "reign of heaven," although he does use "reign of God" in a few places. Since these two expressions are interchangeable in the parallel passages in the Gospels of Mark and Luke, we can conclude that they have the same basic meaning.

Matthew speaks of the Church only twice. In 16:18 the word refers to the Church in general and in 18:17 to a local community. In both instances it suggests some kind of structured organization. It is clear that for Matthew, the reign of heaven and the Church are very closely associated but not identical. The Church lives between the decisive inbreaking of the reign (3:2) and the close of the present age (28:20). The Gospels suggest what the Vatican II's Dogmatic Constitution on the Church (5) states, namely, that the Church is the beginning and the first fruits of the reign of God. According to Matthew's Gospel, the mission of the Church is to establish this reign in the hearts of all people (28:19).

MARK—CHRIST, SON OF MAN, SON OF GOD

One of the major concerns of Mark's Gospel is the question of the true identity of Jesus. The events recorded in the stories that comprise this gospel narrative both reveal facets of Jesus' mysterious personality to those who believe and conceal his identity from those who have no faith. In addition to these narratives, Mark's characterization of Jesus is enhanced through the use of some traditional messianic titles.

Christ

The title *Christ* means "anointed one" and is the Greek equivalent of the Hebrew *Messiah*. Although in ancient Israel both priests and kings were anointed and, consequently, messianic expectations appeared within both groups, the early Christians favored the tradition of a royal messiah over that of a priestly one. The prominence of royal messianism can be seen in the inscription that was nailed to the cross of Jesus, "the King of the Jews" (15:26, 32). Mark would have us believe that while Jesus did accept the title "Christ," he rejected its royal undertones (12:35), and instead associated it with "Son of Man," another messianic tradition (14:62). At the beginning of his Gospel, Mark himself identifies Christ, not as the royal son of David, but as the divine Son of God (1:1).

The account of Peter's confession of Jesus as the Christ (8:29) is a turning point in the Gospel. It signals the transition from the Galilean ministry to the move toward Jerusalem. More importantly, it symbolizes the beginning of the gradual disclosure to the disciples of the true identity of Jesus.

Son of Man

The phrase "son of man" appears first in the Book of Ezekiel, where it underscores the lowliness of a human being as compared to God. As a title, it probably originated in pre-Christian Jewish apocalyptic circles. It is found in the Book of Daniel where "one like a son of man" acts as the agent of God's salvation and judgment (7:13-14). This mysterious individual appears to be more a heavenly being than a human person and, in this guise, embodies a unique messianic expectation. The anticipated royal or priestly messiah was expected to arise from within the respective social group. The Son of Man, on the other hand, would arrive on the clouds of heaven.

"Son of Man" is the title that Mark puts on the lips of Jesus, and only Jesus. It was as Son of Man that Jesus exercised power on earth (2:10, 28); that he would suffer, die, and be raised from the dead (8:31; 9:9, 12, 31; 10:33, 45; 14:21, 41); and that he would finally return in glory (8:38; 13:26; 14:62). In Mark, it is precisely through his humiliation that this heavenly figure triumphs.

Son of God

During the time of the monarchy, this title belonged to the king who was believed to be like a son of the god (see 2 Sam 7:14; Pss 2:7; 89:26-27). However, by the time of Jesus, Greek and Roman religious influences prompted the Jews to revive the title's literal and original meaning. Once again it identified its bearer as some kind of divine manifestation.

The divine sonship of Jesus is attested to by God both at Jesus' baptism (1:11) and at the transfiguration (9:7). When Jesus himself admits that he is "the son of the Blessed One," he is accused of blasphemy (14:61-64). In this Gospel, only the demons know for sure that Jesus is the Son of God and they are ordered to be silent about it (1:24-25; 3:11-12; 5:7). The one person in the entire Gospel who acclaims Jesus as Son of God is the centurion at the cross, and his confession of faith comes after Jesus' death (15:39).

LUKE—POVERTY, MERCY

Luke's Gospel is rich with diverse yet interconnected theological motifs. Chief among them are poverty and mercy. Examining these themes in both the First and the Second Testaments will deepen our appreciation of the theology found in this particular Gospel.

Poverty

The biblical writings show that both the ancient Israelites and the early Christians looked upon an abundance of material possessions and economic security as rewards for individual or national righteousness. Those who were able to acquire and retain these advantages were esteemed as virtuous, while those who, for any reason at all, were dispossessed were scorned as sinful and deserving of their lot.

The primary meaning of the Hebrew word for "poverty" is dependence with the implication of lowliness, and dispossession. In a religious sense it suggests humility or piety. This state of lowliness, distress, incompetence, and worthlessness often, although not always, resulted from circumstances of economic deprivation. But the poverty that is praised is not mere material dependence. It is, rather, a humble reliance on God that often results from, but is not guaranteed by, economic need. It seems that when there were forces within the society which prevented some members from enjoying the prosperity and sense of well-being that rightly belonged to everyone, the poor became the special concern of God (Pss 72:4; 132:15), and the rest of the community had the responsibility of providing for them, not simply out of charity, but out of justice. In this way, God was regarded as the protector of and provider for the poor.

Luke's attention to the poor can be seen in Mary's song (which praises God's concern for the needy) (1:46-55), in the favor shown to the unpretentious shepherds (2:8-14), and in the social message of John the Baptist (3:10-14). Jesus appeals to the preaching of good news to the poor as evidence of his messianic identity (4:18; 7:22). Examples of this teaching include the sermon on the plain with its blessings and woes (6:20-26), the parable of the rich fool (12:16-21), and the story of the dishonest servant (16:1-9).

Mercy

Originally, mercy (or loving-kindness) was associated with the covenant obligation between God and human beings and among human covenant partners themselves. The Gospel of Luke expands the idea of covenant membership and focuses on those people on the fringes of the community: the poor, the lowly, outcasts, women, etc. Jesus shows special concern for these marginal people, consistently showing pity, sympathy, and kindness toward the weaker members of society. He brings the merciful love of God to those who have been forsaken by others. The parable of the Good Samaritan (10:25-37) is a classic example of such love and concern.

Jesus' injunction to be merciful as God is merciful is also found in the sermon on the plain (6:36). It follows his teaching on love of enemies (6:27-35), in which he insists that it is not enough to love those who love us, or to give to those from whom we can expect some return. Such love and such giving are found even in the wicked. Christian love and mercy goes beyond this kind of attachment and loyalty. It is much more than an attitude of mind. It is an active love, a love that, like the merciful love of God, is willing to do good regardless of the cost. Luke insists that those toward whom we show mercy should be precisely those from whom we feel alienated, those with whom we have been in conflict, those who might take advantage of us or from whom we can expect no favor in return. This is the kind of mercy that Jesus shows (5:31-32).

JOHN—WORLD, SIGN

The Gospel of John differs from the other Gospels in both style and content. Here the primary focus is less on the future reign of God than on the unique relationship between Jesus and his Father and the participation of believers in that divine relationship. The life, death, and resurrection of Jesus are recounted from this theological point of view. The Gospel itself can be divided into the Book of Signs (1:19–12:50) and the Book of Glory (13:1–20:31). In the first part, Jesus' miracles are not signs of God's reign, but of Jesus' true identity, which is fully manifested in the second part through his exaltation on the cross.

World

The world is the stage on which the drama of human life unfolds. Judaism held in balance at least two views of the world, namely, that the created world is fundamentally good (Gen 1:31), and that, even so, it is subject to divine judgment (Psalm 9). John understands the world in both ways. The first can be seen in the familiar saying, "God so loved the world that he gave his only son" (3:16). This passage suggests that the world, though clearly in need of salvation, is so cherished that God, who created it through the Word (1:3), is now willing to save it through Christ.

There is a second and perhaps more characteristic way that John speaks of the world. He draws a stark contrast between those who accept Jesus and those who do not (1:10-11). There is no middle group here, no time for indecision. All people, indeed, all of reality belongs to one camp or the other. John pits the world against God just as he pits darkness against light (3:19), falsehood against truth (8:44), death against life (5:24). When "world" is used in this sense, it stands for all that is hostile to God and to the one whom God has sent. This is the world that will face judgment when the Advocate comes (16:8-11).

John also describes the struggles of life as a battle between the kingdom of this world and the reign of God. He claims that Jesus will ultimately conquer the ruler of this world (12:31; 14:30; 16:11) and will draw everyone to himself (12:32). Whether or not John actually viewed reality dualistically, this way of speaking underscores the urgency of deciding for or against Jesus. According to John, to hesitate is to choose the world.

Sign

In John's Gospel, the seven signs of Jesus are clearly miraculous but, more importantly, they bear messianic significance. The wonders themselves do not lead to faith (2:23-25). They point to some aspect of the true identity of Jesus. Four of them are followed by discourses that provide an interpretation of the marvel. Despite this explanation, some bystanders recognize the meaning of the miracle, while others do not.

The changing of water into wine at Cana (2:1-11) symbolizes the replacement of the Jewish ceremonial washing by the work of Jesus. Both the rescue of the son of an official from imminent death (4:46-54) and the cure of the man at the Sheep Gate (5:1-9) demonstrate the healing power of Jesus' word, a power not confined to the restrictions of space. The miraculous feeding of the multitude (6:1-15) and the ensuing walking on the sea (6:16-24) depict Jesus overshadowing the Mosaic traditions of bread in the wilderness (see Exod 16:14-15) and crossing the sea (see Exod 14:21-22). The cure of the man born blind and the consequences of that man's testimony (9:1-34) demonstrate both the power of faith in Jesus and the price that such faith can exact. The raising of Lazarus (11:1-44), the climactic event in the public ministry of Jesus, not only reveals his power over life and death, but also identifies him as the very essence of life eternal.

ACTS—HOLY SPIRIT, GENTILE

Acts of the Apostles is the second of Luke's two-volume work. It traces the expansion of the Christian community which, under the guidance of the Holy Spirit, moved from "Jerusalem, throughout Judea and Samaria . . . to the ends of the earth" (1:8). As the Christian mission moved away from Jerusalem and its Jewish roots to the Gentile world, the prominence of Peter, James, and the Twelve gave way to that of Paul and his missionary companions.

Holy Spirit

This book has frequently been referred to as "the gospel of the Holy Spirit," because within its pages every significant missionary step is taken in response to the inspiration of the Spirit. The followers of Jesus are identified as those who are "baptized with the Holy Spirit" (1:5). This same Spirit enabled them to stand up boldly and witness to the truth as they had experienced it (4:8-12). The Spirit increased their numbers (8:15-17; 19:17; 10:44-45; 11:15; 19:6-7) and provided them with outstanding leaders (Stephen, 6:3, 5; Paul, 9:17; Barnabas, 11:24). According to Luke, the Spirit inspired prophetic teaching about the fulfillment of ancient expectations (1:16; 4:25; 28:25). Acts depicts the Church as the fulfillment of God's promises to Israel's ancestors.

From the outpouring of the Spirit at Pentecost (1:4), to the move into the Gentile world by Peter (10:19; 11:12), to the extensive journeys of Paul (13:2, 4), the Holy Spirit directed the

Christian enterprise. Luke insists that it was the Spirit that provided the disciples with the courage necessary to be witnesses to the risen Lord (7:55). Still, he is less concerned with the transformative effects of the Spirit in the lives of individuals than he is with the growth and development of the Church.

The gift of the Spirit was something upon which the Church could depend, but it was not something over which the Church had control. This is clear both from Peter's defense of his baptism of the Gentile Cornelius (11:1-18) and from the fact that baptism, which the Church could regulate, was not a prerequisite for the coming of the Spirit (10:44-48).

Gentile

The word comes from *gens,* the Latin for "nation," a designation that seldom included Israel. This distinction has roots in the First Testament, where "the nations" refers to the non-Jews (Isa 42:1; Jer 36:2; Ps 2:8).

Many Second Testament scholars are convinced that the Christian movement began as a religious renewal of Judaism. They maintain that the Gentile mission undertaken by Paul and others forced the movement into the broader world before its leaders in Jerusalem were able to plan carefully the strategy for its expansion. Paul's writings are filled with evidence of his struggles with those Christians who insisted that the Gentiles must first convert to Judaism before they could become full members of the Christian community (15:1). This controversy should not be confused with the difficulty the Hellenists had with the Hebrews (6:1), for there were many Greek-speaking converted Jews in the early Church. Nor, strictly speaking, does the Cornelius episode (chap. 10) fit into this category. Cornelius is described as a God-fearer, one who accepted some of the teachings of Judaism and attended the synagogue, but was neither circumcised nor observed the dietary regulations.

The Gentiles for whom Paul was champion seem to have had no previous interest in Judaism. They were converted to the risen Christ. According to the account of the Jerusalem Council found in Acts, this first Church crisis was resolved to everyone's satisfaction. The Gentiles had only to observe a few dietary restrictions and to conform to the community's marriage laws (15:29).

ROMANS—SALVATION, FAITH

The central theme of the Letter to the Romans is stated in the very first chapter. "It [the gospel] is the power of God for the salvation of everyone who believes" (1:16). This statement expresses the fundamental theology of all of Paul's writings: salvation is an act of God, it is offered to Jew and Greek alike, and it comes through faith and not good works.

Salvation

Salvation is a word that has rich religious significance, but it has become almost meaningless in popular usage. It suggests a state of danger with a risk of perishing, a state from which we cannot free ourselves. Today most people are so intent on being self-sufficient that they cannot conceive of themselves in need of being saved by another (except, perhaps, from a burning building or a sinking ship). The ancient Israelites, on the other hand, believed that God had saved them by delivering them from situations of oppression (Exod 14:13-14; Ps 18:1-3). The early Christians embraced this belief and identified salvation with the person and ministry of Jesus. They believed that it was through him that God saved, and that God's reign was established in the world. Although there was a sociopolitical aspect to this notion of salvation, its meaning was expanded to include deliverance from other kinds of peril as well.

According to Paul, sin is the rebellion of the creature against the creator. He argues that, since all have sinned (Rom 3:23), and since death came into the world through sin (5:12), all are under the power of death. However, the good news that Paul preached declares that the reign of grace is stronger than the power of sin and death, and this grace was won for us by Christ Jesus (8:34). It was through Christ's obedience that the alienation from God brought on by Adam's disobedience was ended and salvation became a reality open to all.

Paul actually speaks less about final salvation than about the present justification that saves. "How much more then, since we are now justified by his blood, will we be saved through him from the wrath" (5:9). At the heart of this teaching is the conviction that justification and salvation are the work of God. One cannot accomplish it alone. Rather, "a person is justified by faith apart from works of the law" (3:28).

Faith

Paul insists again and again that by ourselves we are unable to resist our sinful inclinations and, thus, all are subject to the wrath of God. This is true for the Gentiles (1:16-32) as well as for the Jews (2:17-29). Only God's freely given righteousness can save us from our sinful selves. Faith is the open and humble heartfelt acceptance of God's righteousness. It enables us to confess that Jesus is Lord. One is justified by faith in Christ and subsequently saved (10:9-10).

Paul recognized that all people have laws that are intended to insure righteous living, and that each individual has an innate sense of right and wrong that acts as a guide in making moral choices. Being himself a Jew, he also knew well the claims made regarding obedience to the Mosaic Law, specifically the relationship between justification and doing the works of the Law. The distinctiveness of Paul's teaching can be seen in his startling assertion that neither obedience to the Law nor performance of good works can merit salvation. In a way, the Law is irrelevant. It can only identify our transgressions and, in a sense, increase our awareness of our own sinfulness (5:20a). This teaching is not an invitation to libertinism (6:1). It is designed to emphasize the excellence of God's freely given grace, for "where sin increased, grace overflowed all the more" (5:20b). "Justified by faith, we have peace with God through our Lord Jesus Christ" (5:1).

1/2 CORINTHIANS—FLESH, SPIRIT

The Letters to the Corinthians reveal more about Paul than do any other Second Testament works. It is especially in 2 Corinthians that we read of Paul's attachments (2:1-4), his struggles (11:23-29), and his personal transformation (12:1-10). Along with the Letters to the Romans (8:1-17) and to the Galatians (5:13-26), these letters also provide us with insight into Paul's understanding of the struggle between the flesh and the spirit. In some passages it is unclear whether Paul is talking about the Spirit of God or the human spirit. However, such a distinction should not be pressed too far, for a person is spiritual only through the power of the Spirit of God.

The Flesh

Flesh denotes human material corporeality. It is with this meaning that physical suffering is called "a thorn in the flesh" (2 Cor 12:7) and death is described as "destruction of the flesh" (1 Cor 5:5). Although flesh originally referred to what in the human is earthly, weak, and transitory, it soon became an allusion to human limitation (1 Cor 15:50) and an indication of a superficial, if not sinful, manner of living (1 Cor 3:3).

Flesh takes on a decidedly negative meaning when it is set in contrast with spirit. Paul spoke of this contrast between the outer self (corporeality) and the inner self (2 Cor 4:16). He also distinguished between the natural or unspiritual person, who judges according to the standards of the world, and the spiritual person, who judges according to the standards of the Spirit of God. Although still living in the flesh, Paul claimed that he was not carrying on a battle with evil using mere weapons of the flesh. Instead, through faith, he had divine power at his disposal (2 Cor 10:1-6). It is easy to see how a word for creaturely weakness came to have moral connotations as well. When flesh is pitted against spirit, it denotes what is limited or weak, even what is evil or prone toward evil. In this way it came to signify unredeemed human nature. Thus, to live "according to the flesh" is to sin. It is important to note that the antithesis between flesh and spirit is not physical; it is ethical. Paul used another word (*soma*) to refer to the physical human body.

Spirit

The Spirit is the divine power that stands in contrast to everything that is human. When used of human beings, *spirit* refers to the relationship one has with God. To the extent that one is open to God's Spirit and is prompted by that Spirit, one is spiritual. As already mentioned, Paul distinguished between spiritual people and natural or unspiritual people (1 Cor 2:12-15; 3:1-4).

Having received the Spirit of God at baptism, Christians now live "in the Spirit." This does not mean that every Christian is faithful to this way of living (see 1 Cor 3:3). It means that everyone is called to such living. Life in the Spirit is a life in faith (2 Cor 4:13). It is the Spirit of God that empowers the Christian to confess Jesus as Lord (1 Cor 12:3) and to live faithful to this confession.

The power of the Spirit is manifested in the lives of Christians through extraordinary phenomena called *charismata,* or spiritual gifts. These include wisdom, exceptional knowledge, healing, miracles, prophecy, discernment of spirits, and speaking in tongues (1 Cor 12:4-11). All of these gifts and all of the ministries that develop because of them are given to individuals, not for themselves but for the upbuilding of the Church (1 Cor 12:7; 14:4). Still, according to Paul, evidence of the presence of the Spirit is to be found less in miraculous deeds than in ethical living. The "more excellent way" of living "in the Spirit" is the way of love (1 Cor 13:1-13).

GALATIANS—GOSPEL, FREEDOM

Although the word *gospel* is commonly associated with one of the four accounts of the life, death, and resurrection of Jesus (according to Matthew, Mark, Luke, and John), the word itself is found more frequently in the writings of Paul than in the narrative accounts themselves. For him, the word refers to the content of the gospel message rather than to its literary form. The gospel that Paul preached bitterly opposed the teaching of Jewish-Christian missionaries who maintained that both faith in Jesus and conformity to Mosaic Law were necessary for salvation. He insisted, instead, that believers had been set free from the burden of the Law.

Gospel

The gospel is the "good news" preached by Jesus that the reign of God had come in him (see Matt 4:14; Mark 1:15). Jesus himself claimed that this message brought to fulfillment the promise announced by the prophets (Luke 4:16-21; see Isa 61:1-4). This is the "good news" that was revealed by God to Paul (Gal 1:11-12). So decisive was this momentous experience of God and the transformation it accomplished in Paul that it became the source of his apostolic activity. From the very beginning, Paul proclaimed that acceptance of Jesus in faith has replaced adherence to the Law as the ultimate means of salvation.

This teaching placed him in constant conflict with "Judaizers," a name given to "the men from James" (2:12), representatives of the head of the Christian community in Jerusalem. Paul accused them of teaching a different gospel, one that was really not good news at all (1:6-7). As observant Jews, they required fidelity to the Law along with faith in Jesus (3:2). Paul argued that as vital as the Law once may have been, it lost its dominant meaning for salvation with Jesus' life, death, and resurrection. If the Jewish-Christians chose to continue to follow their earlier way of life, Paul would not interfere. However, to require this of Gentile converts was to "pervert the gospel of Christ" (1:7), and to refrain from table fellowship with those who were not circumcised was to undermine the unity of the body of believers (2:11-14).

Freedom

Paul used a distinctive method of interpreting earlier biblical material in his attempt to illustrate his teaching on freedom from the Law. It resembles the midrashic approach later developed by the rabbis and employed even today by many Jewish scholars. (*Midrash*, which comes from the Hebrew word meaning "to search," is a creative adaptation of the biblical material in order to discover new meaning.) Pointing out that Abraham's righteousness by faith (Gen 15:6) preceded his covenantal responsibilities (Gen 17:9), Paul argued for the preeminence of faith over works (Gal 3:6-14).

Paul's gospel of freedom is perhaps best illustrated by the allegory that he developed from the traditions about Abraham's two wives and the sons they bore (4:22-31; see Gen 16–17; 21:1-21). Ishmael is "the son of the slave woman . . . born naturally," while Isaac is "the son of the freeborn through a promise" (4:23). Although in the earlier narratives, Isaac is an ancestor of Israel,

Paul very creatively reversed this tradition. Here, Isaac, the "son of promise" and of a freewoman, becomes the ancestor of those who in faith have accepted a new promise, while Ishmael, the son of a slave and bound by law, becomes the prototype of all those under the Law. Paul pleaded with the Galatians: "For freedom Christ set us free; so stand firm and do not submit again to the yoke of slavery" (5:1). This does not mean that faith in Christ absolves us from lives of righteousness (5:13). It means, rather, that righteousness flows from faith in Christ and is manifested in a life lived in the Spirit (5:16-26).

EPHESIANS—BODY OF CHRIST, TEMPLE OF GOD

In several ancient manuscripts, this letter lacks the identification "to the Ephesians." Its literary style is highly liturgical, quite different from that of letters considered genuinely Pauline. For reasons such as these, many commentators today consider it a kind of cover letter that accompanied other correspondence which was circulated among various early Churches. The letter itself discusses the early Christian teaching about the Church's nature. In it, the author develops several images or metaphors that represent the Church. Among them are "body of Christ" and "temple of God."

Body of Christ

Solidarity among members of the Church, characterized as the body of Christ, also appears in other letters (Rom 12:4-8; 1 Cor 12:12-27). The metaphor itself suggests the interrelatedness of all believers. Each is a member of this body, and bound in a most intimate way to Christ. All are also members of one another, dependent on each other, sharing good fortune as well as ill, knit together by the power of love (4:15-16). Christ is the head (1:22; 4:15; 5:23), the channel through which the life of God flows into the body. It was as head of the body that Christ offered himself for the sanctification of all those joined to him (5:25-27), so that each member might "grow in every way into him who is the head" (4:15). This idea clearly points to Christ's authority over all believers. The letter goes on to show that Christ's authority is actually cosmic in scope. Having been raised from the dead, Christ now sits at God's "right hand in the heavens" as "head over all things" (1:20-23).

It seems that the purpose behind the development of this theme was Church unity. This is stated at the beginning of the letter: "a plan for the fullness of times, to sum up all things in Christ, in heaven and on earth" (1:10). The Church, as body of Christ, is the first step in the accomplishment of this goal. Each member of the body, regardless of how unremarkable his or her role, shares in the common life and glory and contributes to the well-being of the whole (4:11-13), under the headship of Christ. Both the circumcised (Jew) and the uncircumcised (Gentile) are thus reconciled in this one body (2:11-16; 3:6).

Temple of God

After describing the Church as a human body, the author alludes to it as a political body, a household (2:19). Taken from the social conventions of the time, this metaphor suggests an arrangement of human relationships under some form of authority. This leads into the use of another metaphor, the actual house or building (2:20), the "dwelling place [temple] of God in the Spirit" (2:21).

The Letter to the Ephesians is not the first place where the metaphor of a building is found. In 1 Corinthians 3:10-16, Paul described how the apostles were the builders of the structure. In Ephesians the image appears slightly different. Here the apostles, along with the Christian prophets, are the foundation of the building, making it secure and trustworthy.

This metaphor functions in a way similar to that of the body. As Christ is the head of the body, which is the Church, so he is the capstone, or cornerstone, of the edifice, which is the Church (2:20). Since the capstone serves as the crown of the building, the image signifies Christ's preeminence. A cornerstone binds two walls together: thus the metaphor is an apt one to represent the unity the Jews and Gentiles experience in Christ. Finally, this whole structure seems to grow, as does a body (2:21). Envisioning the Church as the dwelling place of God highlights the conviction that the true habitation of God is the community of believers.

PHILIPPIANS/COLOSSIANS/PHILEMON—*KENOSIS,* COSMIC, SLAVERY

Each of these letters states that Paul is writing from prison (Phil 1:13; Col 4:3; Phlm vv. 1, 9, 10, 13, 23). As with most of his correspondence, they address situations within the respective communities that were causing Paul great concern. Having labored successfully to establish each Church, he was anxious lest the Christians deviate from the gospel they had received from him.

Kenosis

Kenosis comes from the Greek word meaning "to empty." In the Letter to the Philippians, Paul urged the Christians to be "united in heart, thinking one thing" (2:2). This suggests that the inner unity of the community was at risk. In order to reestablish their earlier harmony, he placed before them the example of the humility of Christ. Using what was perhaps a well-known Christian hymn (2:6-11), Paul described how it was precisely because of Christ's willingness to be emptied of all divine privilege and to assume the stance of a slave, "becoming obedient to death, even death on a cross," that "God greatly exalted him."

It was this kind of emptying that Paul enjoined upon the community at Philippi (2:5). Their personal quarrels and exclusive cliques would have to dissolve in the face of such humble self-effacement. For the sake of harmony in the community, they too would have to be willing to set aside any claims of privilege in order to serve the common good. Only in this way would they be "one in Christ." This notion of self-emptying after the example of Christ has influenced various forms of Christian asceticism down through the ages.

Cosmic

The Letter to the Colossians was written to refute false teaching that was undermining the faith of the community (2:4, 8). It contains a pre-Pauline hymn (1:15-20) used by the author to argue his point (see Phil 2:6-11). In response to those who were teaching that Christ was not the sole source of salvation, the author traced the cosmic dimensions of Christ's sovereignty, using images reminiscent of the ancient Israelite description of primordial cosmic wisdom (Col 1:18; see Prov 8:22). This line of argument was later used against what the author calls "seductive philosophy" which advocated the primacy of the "elemental powers of the world" (2:4-23). We are not sure whether "elemental powers" refers to the elements of the physical world (earth, air, fire, and water), the constellations of the heavens, or astral deities. It is clear, however, that this author insisted that in all things Christ, and only Christ, is preeminent (1:18-20). He is "the head of every principality and power" (2:10, 15).

Slavery

Slavery was very common in the ancient world. The Israelites both had slaves (Exod 12:44) and in dire straits sometimes sold themselves into slavery (Exod 21:2-11). Men, women, and children became slaves through captivity during war (Josh 9:22-23), because of defaulted debts (2 Kgs 4:10), or because of personal loyalty (Deut 15:16-17). Since deliverance by God from bondage was at the heart of the faith of Israel, their own enslavement was considered an intolerable disgrace (Lev 25:42).

While in prison, Paul converted a runaway slave named Onesimus. Apparently the owner, Philemon, was indebted to Paul, who used this indebtedness to bargain for the slave's safe return. Paul neither criticized the practice of slavery, nor demanded the release of Onesimus. He merely asked that the slave be treated as the Christian brother he had become. In several of his letters, Paul taught that faith in Christ undermines slavery by creating a new set of social relationships. There is no longer a distinction between slave and free (1 Cor 12:13; Gal 3:28). All are children of God and should be treated as such.

1/2 THESSALONIANS—ESCHATOLOGY

The First Letter to the Thessalonians is considered the first of Paul's letters, indeed the earliest writing in the entire Second Testament. The author of the Second Letter also claims to be Paul writing to the same community, but there are indications that this is someone writing under Paul's name to an unknown community. The latter author does this, not to deceive, but to interpret Paul's teaching for a new community. Eschatology emerges as a major theme of both letters.

Eschatology

The word comes from the Greek *eschatos,* meaning "last" and usually referring to time, either the last days of the present age, the time of Christ's return, or the new age itself. The idea of the endtime itself originated in Jewish expectation of God's intervention in history through divine judgment and saving acts. Believing that from the very beginning forces of chaos were at odds with the sovereignty of God, Israel placed its confidence in God's ultimate victory. Allusions to this cosmic battle are found throughout the First Testament (Isa 27:1; Pss 74:12-17; 89:10-11; Job 26:12-13). In these passages it is very difficult, and perhaps unnecessary, to separate national eschatology (concern for the future of Israel) from cosmic eschatology (concern for the future of the world). Personal eschatology (concern for the fate of the individual after death) does not appear until quite late in Israel's history.

Various salvific figures, such as the Messiah (Isa 9:5-6; 11:1-9), the Suffering Servant (Isa 42:1-4; 49:1-7; 50:4-11; 52:13–53:12), the Son of Man (Dan 7:13-14), and Elijah returned (Mal 3:23), came to play an important role in Israel's notion of the endtime. Each in its own way was believed to be the one through whom God would intervene to judge and to save, to establish once and for all the reign of God. The early Christians believed that it was through Jesus that God had intervened to establish the eschatological reign and that, while he had indeed begun this great work of salvation, it would only be brought to completion with his return in glory.

1 Thessalonians 4:13-18 reveals that initially Paul expected to be alive when Christ returned (4:15), even though he was not sure when that event would take place (5:2). However, the death of faithful Christians seems to have caused great unrest within the community. If in baptism they had died with Christ and had risen to a new life, what did these deaths imply? Developing the theme of union with Christ in death and resurrection, Paul declared that

the dead were not disadvantaged. They would, in fact, be the first to join the triumphant Christ. Paul was not concerned to provide a glimpse into the specifics of the future. Instead, he sought both to console those who were grieving the loss of their loved ones and anxious about their fate (4:18; 5:11) and to admonish them to remain steadfast as they themselves awaited the Lord's coming (4:1-12; 5:12-22).

The persecutions to which the early Christians were subject led some to believe that the eschatological Day of Judgment was dawning and the present age was coming to an end. 2 Thessalonians 2:1-17 addressed this false expectation. The author warned the Christians not to be taken in by fraudulent claims of consummation. The final Day of the Lord had not yet arrived. The decisive eschatological battle had not yet been waged. The definitive lawless one had not yet been vanquished (2:3-10). Lest they let up their guard, the faithful were reminded of earlier teaching concerning the hidden nature of this great eschatological day and the consequent vigilance required of them as they awaited it (2:5, see 1 Thess 5:1-12). Paul's eschatology is both realized and expectant. The time of fulfillment is "already but not yet."

1/2 TIMOTHY/TITUS—DEACON, PRESBYTER, BISHOP

These three letters, written to Timothy, the leader of the Macedonian Church, and Titus, the leader at Corinth, are called the "Pastoral Letters," because they address the ongoing management of the Churches established by Paul. Upon founding a Church, Paul appointed ministers who would continue the work that he had begun. These letters provide us insight into early Church leadership.

Deacon

A deacon was one who provided some kind of service. Only gradually did this form of ministry become a specific office in the Church. Tracing the appearance of the word throughout the Second Testament reveals this development. Deacons first appear in Acts 6:1-6 where they are set aside to wait on table. However, they are never described as serving in this way. Instead, Stephen worked signs and wonders and debated points of faith (Acts 6:8-10) and Philip evangelized (Acts 21:8).

In the early letters of Paul, deacons take on a more official character. They are mentioned along with bishops (Phil 1:1). In both 1 Timothy 3:8-13 and Titus 1:5-9 qualifications for the appointment of both deacons and bishop are listed together. Although some commentators have minimized the early Christian leadership positions of women, Phoebe is indeed identified by Paul as "a deacon of the church at Cenchreae" (Rom 16:1). Criteria to which women were to conform is also included in the list of diaconal qualification (1 Tim 3:11). Despite these references, it is only in writings from the post-apostolic age that the status and responsibilities of deacons came to be more specifically delineated.

Presbyter

The early Christian office of presbyters, or elders, stems from a similar institution of Judaism, whose holders exercised both judicial (Deut 25:7-9) and cultic roles (Lev 4:13-15). In the Jerusalem Church they probably constituted a council similar to those of the synagogues, governing along with the apostles (Acts 15:2-23; 16:4). Presbyters were also appointed over missionary Churches (Acts 14:23; 20:17; Titus 1:5). These leaders preached and taught (1 Tim 5:17). It was through the imposition of the hands of the presbyters that Timothy himself was consecrated a leader (1 Tim 4:14). Just as the presbyters were associated with the apostles in the Jerusalem Church, they were linked with bishops in some of the Pauline Churches (Titus 1:5-9; see Acts 20:28). These various references indicate the fluid nature of Church order in early Christian times.

Bishop

The word comes from the Greek *episkopos* meaning "overseer," and suggests the pastoral role of caring for or guarding.

From this arises the image of the bishop as a shepherd. The qualifications for a bishop found in both 1 Timothy 3:2-7 and Titus 1:5-9 suggest that management of the material resources of the community was a major responsibility of the office. However, the bishop also had to "be able to exhort with sound doctrine and to refute opponents" (Titus 1:8). Like the deacon, the bishop was initially identified by the service he rendered and not by the office he held although there seems to have been an impulse in this direction from the outset (Acts 20:28).

Bishops were not itinerant preachers. They were leaders of established communities. Since many if not most of these early communities were house-churches, the ability to manage his own household would be considered a requirement for one who aspired to manage the household of the Lord (1 Tim 3:4-5). This role of leadership was necessary both for good order within the community and as a witness of harmonious living to those outside of the community.

HEBREWS—HIGH PRIEST

Although traditionally it has been classified as a letter, this book lacks the literary characteristics of an epistle and is really more of a series of arguments followed by exhortation. Using a form of rabbinic argument known as "from the lesser to the greater" (see, e.g., Luke 23:31), the author attempts to show the superiority of Christ (1:4; 7:7, 19, 22), his covenant (8:6), his sacrifice (9:23), and the benefits he accrues (10:34). It is probably this recurring reference to the Hebrew tradition that gained the document its name. This feature has also led some scholars to identify the addressees as Jewish-Christians who were tempted to return to their ancestral faith. However, the identity of the addressees remains obscure, as does the authorship.

High Priest

The title *high priest* was not used before the Exile. It is first found in the Holiness Code (Lev 21:10). Once the monarchy disappeared, much of the royal paraphernalia was appropriated by the high priest (Zech 6:9-15). By the time of the Hasmoneans (142–63 B.C.E.), the high priest had become the head of the nation as the king had been in days gone by.

The high priest traced his descent from Eleazar the son of Aaron. It is within that tradition that we find a description of high priestly duties, most important of which were the ceremonies of the Day of Atonement. On that occasion he, and only he, would enter the holy of holies and sprinkle the mercy seat with the blood of the sin offerings. He would do this not only for himself but for all the people as well (Lev 16:1-25). He was also required to make atonement for his sins and for the sins of others. This was done by sprinkling the blood of other sin offerings on the veil of the sanctuary and then applying some of it to the horns of the altar (Lev 4:3-21).

The high priests most frequently mentioned in the Second Testament are Annas and Caiaphas (Matt 26:3, 57; Luke 3:2; John 11:49; 18:13-28; Acts 4:6). They were disdained by the Christians because of their involvement in the passion of Jesus and the persecution of Peter and John. Presuming knowledge of the early religious tradition and the more recent history, the author of Hebrews set out to show that Christ is the divinely appointed high priest of the new covenant (2:17; 3:1).

Since Jesus did not descend from Aaron, it was necessary to establish the legitimacy of his priesthood in another way. This is done by identifying him as Son of God (4:14) who, like the mysterious Melchizedek (7:1-17; Gen 14:18-20), had neither beginning nor end. The author concludes his priestly representation of Christ by juxtaposing two messianic references (5:5f.; see Pss 2:7; 110:4) and claiming that Christ fulfills what they merely intimated.

Jesus was like the high priests of old, in that he identified with the entire people. Nevertheless, he was "holy, innocent, undefiled, separated from sinners, higher than the heavens," and unlike them, he had no need to offer sacrifice for himself. In fact, his sacrifice *of* himself expiated all sin once for all (7:26-28). Christ gained for us eternal redemption (9:12), eternal inheritance (9:15), and forgiveness of sin (10:18). Thus he not only fulfilled the cultic requirements, he transcended them.

The high priests of old had access to the holy of holies, but Christ, and Christ alone, had access to God's heavenly throne of glory (4:14). Once he entered it, our great high priest won access to the sanctuary for us as well. Now, cleansed through the sprinkling of his blood, we too can confidently approach God (10:19-23). By insisting on the excellence of the new sanctuary over the old one, the author once again argues for Christ's preeminence.

JAMES/1/2 PETER/JUDE—WORKS, NEW BIRTH, HERESY

These letters, along with those of John, were referred to by early Church writers as the "Catholic (or General) Letters," because they were written either to a general audience or to unidentifiable individuals. Although this designation is not entirely accurate (1 Peter is addressed to several Churches in Asia Minor and 3 John to Gaius), it has persisted. The letters are probably pseudonymous, each book claiming some kind of apostolic authority.

Works

The Letter of James contains much *paraenesis* or moral exhortation, concerned primarily with social obligation within the community. The author seems to have been in conflict, not with Paul who insisted on justification by "faith apart from works of the law" (Rom 3:28), but with those who held that good works were not necessary if one had faith. This is not a struggle between faith and works; it is a corrective. It advocates what has been called "active faith," claiming that faith not manifested through good works is dead (2:17). Like a good rabbinic teacher, this author argues from earlier traditions, specifically the examples of Abraham, who showed his faith in his willingness to sacrifice Isaac (Gen 22:1-14), and Rahab, whose good works gained her protection from the invading Israelite armies (Josh 2:1-21). James's argument shows how even the best theology (e.g., justification by faith) can result in a distortion if it is not understood properly.

New Birth

First Peter seems to be a pastoral exhortation directed to newly baptized Christians who found themselves aliens and sojourners

(1:1; 2:11) in a world to which they once belonged. The author explains that if they felt marginal to society it was because they had been given "a new birth to a living hope" (1:3). They were like newborn infants who must become accustomed to fresh milk (2:2), like stones that make up a new building (2:4-6), like a new people who have received God's merciful love (2:10). Their new life, though it may have seemed fragile, would provide them with the strength they needed to endure the persecutions that some of them were facing (4:12-19). They were admonished to be faithful to the new way of life that was theirs (2:11-3:7), to live lives that bore witness to the faith that was theirs (3:8f.), and to "always be ready to give an explanation to anyone who asks you for a reason for your hope" (3:15).

Heresy

The word, meaning "separate teaching," comes from the Greek word for "sect." In the Jewish community, both the Sadducees and the Pharisees were called sects (Acts 5:17; 15:5; 26:5) as were the Christian themselves (Acts 24:5, 14; 28:2). When sects existed within the Christian communities, they tended to be divisive and were thus condemned (1 Cor 11:19; 2 Pet 2:1). Both 2 Peter and Jude seem anxious about teaching that endorsed sectarian behavior that perverted the grace of God (2 Pet 2:2; Jude 4).

Jude attacked the immoral behavior of the sects rather than their perverted thinking. Alluding to traditions found in apocryphal Jewish works, he provided his readers with examples of other incidents of immorality and the dire punishment they occasioned. 2 Peter addressed the question of God's ability to judge the world by condemning both libertinism and skepticism about the endtime. The "scoffers" (3:3) tried to justify their immorality by challenging the hope of Christ's return in glory, claiming that since he had not yet come, the rigors of Christian morality were absurd. In response, 2 Peter, like Jude, included traditional examples of divine judgment passed against immorality (2:4-16), showing that God intervened in history before, and would do so again.

1/2/3 JOHN—ANTICHRIST, LOVE, HOSPITALITY

Traditionally these letters have been ascribed to John the son of Zebedee, who is thought to have written the Fourth Gospel and the Book of Revelation. There appears to have been division within the Johannine community over the proper understanding of the humanity of Jesus. Each of these letters was written to deal with some challenge to the teaching or authority of its writer.

Antichrist

The antichrist is the rival of God's messianic purpose, a demonic or demonic-human adversary of Christ who will appear before Christ's final coming in glory. Although the antichrist tradition has a long and involved history (see Dan 11:36f.; 2 Thess 2:3-4), the term itself appears only in these letters. Knowledge of the eschatological character of this tradition is presumed by the author of 1 John, who interpreted the appearance of antichrists in the community as evidence of the arrival of the last hour (2:18; 4:3). These antichrists are identified as those who were members of the community but had apostatized and were denying that Jesus had "come in the flesh" (1 John 2:22; 4:2f.; 2 John 1:7). In the spirit of the antichrist, they rejected the doctrines of the incarnation and the redemption, denying both the Son and the Father (1 John 2:23). Thus the antichrist, though an apocalyptic figure of the future, was already at work in these false teachers.

Love

The eschatological struggle is between the children of God and the children of the devil (1 John 3:10), that is, those prompted by the spirit of the antichrist. Here the designation "children of God" does not refer merely to the baptized, for the false teachers also had belonged to the community. Instead, one is begotten of God through faith in Jesus who is the Christ (1 John 5:1) and this faith manifests itself in love (1 John 4:7). From this flows the double commandment to believe and to love (1 John 3:23). The command to love is not a new one (1 John 2:7; 3:11). What is new is the declaration that "God is love" (1 John 4:8), and that we love because God first loved us (1 John 4:19). We know this love through Jesus' laying down his life for us (1 John 3:16). "If God so loved us, we also must love one another." This admonition to love is repeated throughout 1 John (2:3-5, 7-11; 3:11, 18, 23; 4:7, 11, 21) and found also in 2 John (5).

If the humanity of Jesus (1 John 2:22; 4:2f.; 2 John 7) is denied, then so is redemption through his blood (see 1 John 1:7). If the foremost sign of God's love (i.e., Jesus' sacrifice [3:16]) is empty of meaning, then God's love is itself in doubt. These are the errors that the author confronted.

Hospitality

The custom of extending hospitality, a necessity in the desert, became a virtue among travelers. Guests were guaranteed protection, lodging, and provisions (Job 31:32; Gen 18:1-8). Acceptance of hospitality even reconciled enemies. The early Churches were admonished to extend hospitality (Rom 12:13; 1 Tim 3:2; Titus 1:8; Heb 13:2; 1 Peter 4:9), and the missionaries took advantage of this well-established custom (Matt 10:11-15; Acts 16:14-15).

Third John, addressed to a certain Gaius, was written in an attempt to secure hospitality and material support for traveling missionaries (5-8). The author had written first to an unnamed community but, because of a certain Diotrephes, hospitality had not been extended (10). In contrast, the unnamed lady to whom 2 John was written was advised to refuse hospitality to any apostate, described by the author as a deceiver and the antichrist (2 John 7-11; 1 John 2:18-23), since to show hospitality would suggest acceptance of his or her teaching.

REVELATION—SERPENT, SATAN, DEVIL

"The huge dragon, the ancient serpent, who is called the devil and satan, who deceived the whole world, was thrown down to earth" (Rev 12:9). This description of the enemy of God is a combination of mythological features derived from independent sources that originally had little or no reference to each other. Three major images, the serpent or dragon, the devil, and satan, gradually merged into one, creating the picture of *the* "evil one."

Serpent

In the ancient Near Eastern myth of creation, a young, brave warrior-god goes to battle with the destructive forces of chaos represented as a dragon or serpent of the sea. The image became a classic symbol for primordial or fundamental evil and appears throughout the literature of the area, including the Bible. The ever-present struggle between the forces of good and the forces of evil is described as the slaying of the dragon (Isa 27:1; 51:9; Pss 74:13f.; 89:11) or the harnessing of the power of the sea (Matt 8:26; Mark 4:39; Luke 8:24). The threatening sea will only be destroyed at the end of time (Rev 21:1).

The serpent was also a symbol of fertility in the cults that grew up in worship of it. What was a sign of life in these practices became for Israel a sign of evil. Thus the image symbolized both primordial wickedness and cultic perversion.

Satan

Common in the Second Testament, the word is only found in post-Exilic books of the First Testament, and then in juridical settings. In Hebrew the word means "adversary," and suggests a judicial prosecutor or accuser at law. In the Book of Job he fulfills a heavenly governmental role and appears in the court of heaven with the "sons of God" (1:6; 2:1; the same picture is found in Zech 3:1f.). There he neither tempts nor generates wickedness himself. Rather, he tests God (1:11; 2:5) and, with God's permission (1:12; 2:6), he afflicts Job (1:13-19; 2:7f.). Only gradually does the satan change from being the prosecutor of evil to being the perpetrator of misfortune. In the account of David's temptation (1 Chr 21:1), the word appears without the article, indicating that what was once considered a role (the adversary) had become a proper name (Satan).

Devil

A kind of dualism was introduced into Israel's world view when it encountered Persian thought. There the perennial struggle between good and evil was attributed to the influence of angels and demons who held sway over various regions of the universe. Israel assimilated this apocalyptic view, replacing Angra Mainyus, the chief of the hostile kingdom, with the devil, and Ahura Mazda, the agent of light and goodness in Persian thought, with Michael, the guardian angel of Israel (Dan 10:13, 21; 12:1) and chief of the forces of heaven.

As Israel struggled with evil, its origin, and its influence, concepts which variously expressed different dimensions of the reality gradually merged and crystallized around one central figure that possessed a variety of names and descriptions. This convergence took place in pre-Christian Judaism and would have been known at the time of Jesus and of the later Christian community from which the Book of Revelation arose. To this amalgam of traditions were added others which, though totally unrelated, are poetic or symbolic expressions of some aspect of evil. Examples include the sin of the angels with human women (Gen 6:1-4) and Lucifer's fall from heaven (Isa 14:12). Because Revelation speaks of the final conquest by the victorious lamb, all these symbolizations of evil are brought together in this description of the ultimate eschatological victory.

Index

The Bible Today

- **In your ministry**
- **For your spirituality**
- **For its scholarship**

Professionals or para-professionals seeking a deeper, richer knowledge of God's Word will enjoy this award-winning magazine. *The Bible Today* offers the very latest information on Scripture from the most recent and best biblical scholarship. It explores Scripture through illustrated articles and commentary that focus on how the Bible and biblical scholarship can address contemporary concerns. Published six times a year in understandable and instructive language, *The Bible Today* is ideal for individual or group study of the Bible.

Features

Puzzling Passages
Each issue is dedicated to examining a notoriously difficult passage from the Bible. You are provided with a brief description of the problems related to the text and suggestions on how to solve the puzzle.

The Bible On . . .
Biblical scholars explore how the biblical tradition can shed light on contemporary concerns.

Announcements
Announcements alert you to workshops, tours, or other scripture study related events.

Seers' Corner
Beautifully illustrated text helps you experience for yourself important events, people and places of the ancient and modern biblical world.

The Bible in Ministry
This feature helps you discover ways of using the Bible responsibly and effectively in your ministry.

Book Reviews
Book reviews offer you a wealth of information on recent books.

For more information or to place an order
CALL 1-800-858-5450 • FAX 1-800-445-5899